Also by Stuart Kahan

For Divorced Fathers Only

The
Expectant
Father's
Survival Kit

by Stuart Kahan

MONARCH

PUBLISHED BY MONARCH
A SIMON & SCHUSTER DIVISION OF
GULF & WESTERN CORPORATION
SIMON & SCHUSTER BUILDING
1230 AVENUE OF THE AMERICAS
NEW YORK, NEW YORK 10020

DESIGNED BY DAVID NETTLES
MANUFACTURED IN THE UNITED STATES OF AMERICA

1 2 3 4 5 6 7 8 9 10

LIBRARY OF CONGRESS CATALOGING IN PUBLICATION DATA
KAHAN, STUART.
    THE EXPECTANT FATHER'S SURVIVAL KIT.

    INCLUDES INDEX.
    1. PREGNANCY.   2.   FATHERS.   I.   TITLE.
RG525.K18   612.6'3   77–17919
ISBN 0–671–18345–1

For Nancy, who made this all possible

Contents

Introduction

Chapter 1   **MONTHS 1, 2, & 3**   **5**

How to cope with initial reactions
Finding an obstetrician
What to read
Old wives' tales
Mental effects on you
Sex and you: Part 1
Your new physical problems
Her nutrition and your stomach

Chapter 2   **MONTHS 4, 5, & 6**   **57**

Clothes 'n' things
The cash flow
More physical changes
Sex and you: Part 2
Positions
Exercising
Naming the baby
Methods of delivery

Chapter 3   **MONTHS 7, 8, & 9**   **97**

Anxiety attacks
Sex and you: Part 3

Contents

Moving around
Natural childbirth
Obstetrical terms
Genetics
Organizing the home
Labor: At the hospital
Delivery: By yourself
B-Day

Chapter 4   **THE 10TH MONTH**   **165**

Feelings of becoming a father
The baby and you

Index   **177**

Expecting Anticipating the coming or occurrence of

> —*Webster*

Fatherhood To accept the responsibility for

> —*Webster*

Survival Continuing longer than another thing

> —*Webster*

and

I have a headache

> —*Otto Salamon*

Introduction

I was sitting at my desk shuffling invoices from left to right when the phone call came in.

"Guess what?"

That was all it took. With those two magic words, my life was to be altered dramatically. At the age of thirty-eight, I was about to experience pregnancy for the first time. What I felt at that point was a mixture of happiness, panic, curiosity, bewilderment, satisfaction, and shock, a blend strong enough to send me off to Mars if I swallowed a match, lighted or not.

I turned to the library for help as to what I could expect during the coming months. All of the books which had been written on pregnancy were of no use. Most of them seemed to contain at least one lovely picture of mother and baby, suitable for framing, but the guy who started it all was relegated to the background.

Don't get me wrong. Much of this may have been unintentional simply because no one had ever stepped forward with any information we men could relate to. Therefore, to say that the information imparted in these books was sketchy, insofar as the male was concerned, would be an understatement.

For example, you could find one book containing 1,653 pages of rather fine print and on page 575 would come the first direct reference to the male, something to the effect that the man, during this important period, must be able to comfort and help the expectant mother so that she will realize a fulfilled and happy delivery.

Another book would devote one chapter to the man's role, even though it would be only eleven pages and in print geared for reading by far-sighted monkeys. Oh, eight pages of that chapter would be photographs.

Other books would have similar reminders to the male, perhaps referring to his role as that of helper, not too dissimilar from the honeybee's in making the Queen Bee her home. Or they may simply tell him that he must understand fully the complexity of the female's plight. Yes, plight!

If the books on the market today cover anything about men, they blanket it in high-sounding phrases, fifty-dollar words, and a wealth of excess verbiage. Things, however, are beginning to change. Men are becoming more and more involved in what is happening in all aspects of today's society, and they are realizing that the creation of a new human being is just as much their responsibility as the woman's.

One book which is typical of that new concept is *Preparing for Parenthood* by Dr. Lee Salk, who is Director of Pediatric Psychology at New York Hospital in New York City.

He says that "since fathers are equally as important as mothers in child rearing, I feel that it is absolutely essential for males to be actively involved. And the best way to get father psychologically involved is right from the start, which means at the time pregnancy is confirmed."

Studies have shown that men are doing exactly that. They are getting more involved; they want to know what is happening and they are trying to experience as much as they can. Pregnancy is no longer a unilateral movement.

It is important, therefore, that we males consider where we fit into this picture and what we can do. And there is plenty to do. Women have a plethora of information available. They know what to expect at any given time and what to do about it. What we need then is something *we* can relate to.

Why? Because we have our own pregnancy. It's true. Maybe not to the extent of the women, but we go through our own pains and pop our own pills. You name it, we can have it—and most of the time we do.

During the months of my own pregnancy, I gathered information about the kinds of things men usually experience and I tried to find out ways in which different men have handled them. This book is intended to show you what you can do about those pains and pills, how best to handle certain situations, what to expect, what to say, and how to say it.

One thing should be understood. I am not telling you that the experiences are universal among all men, but to the many I have spoken to, similar moments have been shared. In this book, you will be exposed to everything from the changes in the bedroom (and what you can do about it) to the changes in your (and I mean *your*) physical and mental well-being. There is even a section which will help you deliver your own baby in an emergency.

It is true that while we men ride the train to that brief-case and lunchbox castle in the sky, the women are at home (or at the office) letting out their waistbands in between

3

bouts of morning sickness. You would normally think that we had the easier of the two roads. You would, eh? Did you ever see a man's face when that mind-boggling call comes in?

"Harvey, I'm pregnant!"

Chapter 1:
Months 1, 2, & 3

In a remote part of southern India, when the mother-to-be goes into labor, the father-to-be also lies down. No, change that. He doesn't just lie down. He stays flat on his back in the cool shade of his tent while most of the women in the village tend to his needs. They feed him, they bathe him, they comfort him. His cup runneth over.

The wife? Oh, she is off somewhere else (probably in the forest) giving birth to the baby.

This was just one man's way of coping with becoming a father. It is known as "couvade," which comes from the French *couver*, "to hatch." In effect, it is a sympathetic sharing in the pain of childbirth. But, that's only at the end of the nine-month period, at the time of delivery. Can you imagine what went on when he first learned his wife was pregnant?

How to Cope with Initial Reactions
"Guess Who's Coming to Stay?"

Many men experience empathy with the woman at the very beginning, ranging from backaches to morning sickness, from heartburn to varicose veins. Of course, these are only the physical symptoms. The initial emotional reactions of most men when they hear of their impending fatherhood are pretty much the same. For example, my reaction to the news that I was to be a father was a combination of many feelings; some bubbling on the surface, some fermenting well beneath. Most of these, however, were really anchored by the feeling known as Fear; that is, not knowing what was going to happen.

Everybody knows somebody who has gone through the nine-month regime, but somehow when it is happening to you, things take on a different perspective.

Most of the time we men pretty much can clue into what is, or will be, taking place. The time of surprises has long since past. Remember those movies of the 1940s where the poor Dagwood-type husband was the last to know? There he is, sitting in his favorite wingback chair, reading the evening comics while she sits opposite him knitting. Night after night, she knits. She is halfway through a pink sweater and has already gained fifteen pounds before he looks up and asks what she is doing. She tilts her head to one side and gives him a coy smile, at which point the fluorescent bulb in his head flickers on. He drops the paper and sinks to all fours. The serenade begins. He wants her to sit down immediately and put her feet up. (She's already sitting down with her feet propped on a hassock.)

He begins foaming at the mouth, stuttering and running around gathering footballs and baseballs and hockey pucks. In short, he has become a blithering imbecile.

Unless you're living a movie, that doesn't really happen. Nine times out of ten, your wife will wake one morning complaining of nausea. She will have a bloated feeling, and may have just missed her second period. She will tell you that she is going to have it "all checked out" although she has an inkling what this is. Something "must be brewing." Chances are you too have an inkling of what is going on, unless, of course, you are on the U.S.S. *Chipmunk* en route to the Fiji Islands for the next two years. In fact, you may have even planned the baby or you may have talked about it in generalities. It doesn't matter. Surprises, as we remember from those movies, do not really exist, even with a wife who says "Let me be the first to congratulate you."

My baby wasn't exactly planned, at least not consciously. Nancy (my wife) and I spoke about the possibility of having one, certainly before I reached forty and she turned thirty-five, but with each of us earning good wages and enjoying our freedom, it seemed that the last thing we needed was responsibility in the form of an infant. So, when she said she was going to a clinic to take a test, I didn't listen. Somehow, I put that piece of information away in the secondhand drawer of my mind and promptly left it there. After all, she was a career woman earning almost as much as me. A baby would be okay, I guess, but let's wait another year, or two, or three, or. . . .

When the call came in, though, I was speechless. I could barely think. But, you know, somehow the years of the movies, magazines, and television commercials had taken their toll in some small measure. And perhaps what I did really told how I felt.

Don't misunderstand me. I didn't believe in the typical male reaction characterized by Cary Grant-like movements: jumping in the air like a chimpanzee, clicking heels like Pat Rooney and running from one end of the room to the other whistling "California Here I Come" Jolson-style. No sir. Calmly and most decisively, I left the office.

I stopped at the corner and bought my wife a bunch of daisies. I then headed for the nearest Woolworth's where I purchased the biggest stuffed St. Bernard I could find. It set me back $19.98, plus tax. Oh, for the expected baby, I got a rattle.

The initial feelings then that one experiences when told there is a baby en route cover a broad spectrum. No one can ever say he has a monopoly on reactions.

Men are sometimes criticized for their failure to react in a certain, stereotyped way, or they are criticized for so acting in such a stereotyped way. Most of these criticisms come from the women who believe men lack sensitivity. Let's face it. The male makeup is quite different from the female. We may have many of the same fears and concerns but the degree each fear and concern is given differs sharply. Where a woman might burst into tears on learning she is pregnant, a man might turn pale and reach for something to keep him upright. He is bombarded by internal questions:

Will I be a good enough parent? What do I have to do to be a good parent? Am I too old? Am I too young? What kind of responsibilities will I have? What happens to my relationship with my wife, mistress, or other? Will the child even like me? Will I do the same thing to my child as my parents did to me?

These questions nag at you, and they are quite common. For example, a first-time father at the age of thirty-one was particularly concerned over that last one:

"My father did nothing for me. I rarely even saw him. I didn't know what he would do if he was home long enough to really see me. He always seemed to be out of the house. It was as if he was purposely trying to ignore me. I don't know why. Maybe he was afraid. But, I don't really care any more. I just want to make sure I don't behave that way to my kid."

Another prospective father, age twenty-six, was less concerned with the way he would act toward his child than how it would react to him:

"What if the baby doesn't like me? It's possible, isn't it? Look, he could only like his mother. Where would that leave me?"

And then, there are those who challenge their relationship with the mother-to-be; witness this father-to-be at age forty:

"We've been married for twelve years now. It's been a good marriage. I'm just hoping this doesn't change it. You know what I mean? She's liable to turn all her attention to the new one. I guess I'm somewhat inse . . . uh, secure . . . after twelve years but still . . ."

Approaching fatherhood can also trigger all sorts of offbeat reactions, ranging from severe depression to delusions of grandeur. However, if you are able to answer the questions which concern you, to your satisfaction, or get them out in the open where they could at least be answered, then you should be able to recognize that you are probably very proud of what you have accomplished. And fatherhood is an accomplishment.

Look at yourself in the full-length mirror. Flex a muscle here. Another one there. Smile at the image. Puff out your chest. Now you're cooking. Who has time to think about crying, to think about depression? Who? I'll tell you who. Drop your hands to your sides. Dip into your pockets. Anything in there?

Ah, the second wave of feelings arise. How do I pay for all this? How do I support this expanded family? What if the baby gets sick? What if I get sick? How fragile is the baby anyway? Where do I find the money to pay for the doctors and the hospital and for the pills and the crib and what about the shoes and the orthodontist and the college and the wedding present and the grandchildren's birthdays and . . . ?

Let's see, if I can save that amount over there for the next six years, and put away that sum sitting there, and if I could get another job to supplement my supplementary job, and if I could eat lunch only every other day, then, and only then, would I have enough to buy that bottle of Natalins.

See how quickly things run away from you? Okay now, go ahead and cry. This concern of yours has been freely translated into one word: Panic!

Sometimes, it will seem like a dream; sometimes, a nightmare. Besides the money, look at what happens to your life. If you have been accustomed to your freedom, in whatever form it has taken, it will obviously unsettle you to realize that such freedom may no longer be available. You cannot go and do as before. You will be more aware there is another person involved, and you will quickly see that your life will now become divided into three sections: without child, semi-with-child (the pregnancy period), and fully-with-child.

Up to this point, you could go where you like and when you like, sleep whenever you feel the urge, watch television when you want, don't watch it when you want; however, those days will end in less than nine months. There will be another person to care for, someone who can't talk and can't walk and can't feed itself. Someone who will depend on you for just about everything.

That can be a little hard to swallow. So, when the great announcement is made and you become part of that world of the nine-month syndrome, your responses to what will be going on around you, inside you, and to you, are crucial. You will have to juggle many thoughts, many feelings, many procedures, and many people. Not only will you be

10

called upon to handle influences from the outside, but you will have to handle what's going on from within, and that's no easy task.

All right then, let's get to the starting gate and the first concern.

Yourself

What it comes down to is this: You are going to have a whole host of things to go through and the only way to find the answers you need is to go out and get them. No one can really do it for you, not if you want to come out of this with any sort of individualism and sanity. How? First, talk to the gal who's in this with you. Let her know your fears. Maximize your discussions with her and minimize your discussions with others.

The questions I was confronted with ranged over a wide area, starting with my age. Was thirty-nine too old to be a father? The answer, at least for me, was no. Neither chronologically nor emotionally. By the same token, I have a friend who is forty-eight expecting his fifth child. Too old for him? Not on your life. He enjoys each new experience as a "natural part of living."

Much depends not only on your chronological age but also on your emotional age. You don't have to act as if you're forty when you're only twenty, but you don't have to act as if you're ten when you're only forty.

There are some, no matter what their age, who cannot entertain the thought of a baby. No one can say this is abnormal. Some men just do not want a baby and there is nothing wrong with this. Who says you have to father children? It is a personal, very personal feeling, but studies have shown that a goodly number of men refrain from becoming parents simply because there are too many unanswered questions. Some studies have even shown that a man's desire for children is primarily his desire to extend himself—a chance as it were at the famed ring of immortality.

The interesting factor in all this is that many of the expectant fathers harbor the same fears and by far the greatest is that of the unknown; in other words, not knowing what to expect. You experience a sense of helplessness, a seeming incapacity to understand a situation. I have already set forth some of the questions which feed this helplessness. The answers may be obtained just by talking them out with your mate. Some of them may require additional help. Don't be afraid to ask for it. There are plenty of competent psychiatrists, psychologists, and marriage counselors around to aid you, plus your own family doctor and your own priest, minister, or rabbi. Actually, anyone you can turn to for objective advice.

Books about babies are all over the marketplace and I have included some recommendations later in this section.

The important thing to remember is to take *positive action*. Don't just sit in the background reacting to everything that happens around you. That's a defensive position and over the long nine-month haul, it would be like trying to contain the Pittsburgh Steelers for eighteen quarters.

So, if you are to become a true partner in this creation of a child, your child, then it is up to you to take as active a part as possible. It is equally important for you to seek out answers to the questions which may be nagging you, not only those about yourself but also those about the things that are affecting you. Why? Because they have an effect not only on you but on those around you.

In her book, *Fathering*, Maureen Green writes:

. . . a man's influence over the life of his child can start long before the fact of birth. The excitement and affection, or lack of both, at the time of conception, the thoughts and actions of the father on hearing of the pregnancy, all influence the mother's attitude to her coming child.

How do you start getting the answers? First, you need to have specific questions, the ones that apply primarily to you. Try this approach. Go down to the basement (or into the study). Close the door. Set up a chair and table. Sit down. Now, make a list, a soul-searching list of your feelings, your fears, your concerns; in other words, the problem areas. It may be one of the most difficult things you can do, to be honest with yourself, but if you really want to understand, you'll do it.

Some of the answers you need may be found in the following pages. For instance, if the lack of money is one of your main problems, turn to pages 22 and 64. If you don't find what you want within these pages, then try some of the sources I've mentioned.

Those Around You

After you have had a chance to look at your own feelings and reactions, you will have to confront (and sometimes combat) those of other people. When the news begins to spread, you will find all sorts of reactions from all sorts of parties. Most people will be excited about the pregnancy, which will afford you some measure of reinforcement and reaffirmation. The majority of the people will be happy, but be ready for diversity: reactions may be as different as bagels are from hot-cross buns.

For example, take parents. Your mate's parents. Much depends on the ethnic, regional, and cultural heritage of the parties. For a working woman from an Irish background, a telephone conversation with her mother may go as follows:

"Mom, I have some good news for you."

"You got a promotion."

"No, not quite."

"You're moving out of that dingy apartment and buying a house in the country?"

"No, also not quite."

"Are you sure it's good news?"

"Oh yes."

"You're not pregnant, are you?"

That's one reaction and you, my friend, will obviously be blamed for this predicament.

If your mother is like my mother and you come from a Jewish or Italian background, the conversation may sound like this:

"Hello, Ma. I have some news for you."

"Waaa . . . Waaa . . . Waaa . . ."

That was it. On those six words alone the dam burst.

Reactions of parents take on different characteristics, too, depending on your rank in the family. Are you the oldest, youngest, or in between? If, for instance, you are the eldest child (like me), the following will probably occur:

First, there will be unbridled joy that Number One Son has finally come through. Father will strut around and begin his collection of dolls. You see, he has already determined from the mystical powers of Eastern Siberia that the baby will be a girl. (These mystical powers are discussed in Chapter 3.)

Your mother will be questioning your wife on a daily basis as to how much weight has been gained. If your mother is anywhere near the norm, she will have married when she weighed a mere eighty-five pounds, ballooned to a hefty one hundred and fifteen carrying you, stayed within five or ten pounds of that with your brothers and now, for

14

reasons known only to Health Spas Incorporated, she has mushroomed to her present fighting weight of one hundred and sixty-five, which doesn't exactly rest that well on a 5'2" frame.

Accordingly, no daughter-in-law will be able to evade the daily interrogation: "So, how much did you gain this week?" The daughter-in-law is not going to like it and she's going to tell you about it. So be prepared.

If, on the other hand, you're the youngest in the family, then you may have to contend with a whole host of different reactions (especially from *your* mother) which cover a wide area, ranging from gloom to jealousy to babyness. Remember, you're still your mother's little boy—and this goes for an only child too.

What can you do about all of this? Actually, not much. The most effective way I have found is to keep your distance. Try to be objective. Don't take things too personally, even if they start talking about how to toilet-train the new edition. I know that's easy to say and quite difficult to follow, but for your own sanity, you may have to take such an approach. You will have other more important things to occupy your time during these next months. No need to get embroiled in someone else's problems even if they do belong to the parents. If you don't handle their reactions in an objective way, you might find yourself thrust into confrontations which might not only split you and your mate, but might just split you as well.

Thus, you've got yourself starring in a balancing act. Juggle well. Oh, one other thought. It is vitally important never to tread on a mother's feelings. Remember, she's also a potential baby-sitter.

Friends, though, are a different kettle of fish. They'll give you fewer problems, at least not as demanding as the ones

15

from the parents. Basically, friends break down into specific groups: the marrieds, the soon-to-be marrieds, the singles, and the soon-to-be singles.

The marrieds are probably the ones happiest over your situation. However, you should understand the reason why. This happiness translates into: "Good, now you're one of us. Now you'll be able to understand what we have gone through: the late night feedings, the colds, the coughs, the baby-sitters, the teething, the screaming, the braces on the teeth, the summer camps, the poison ivy . . . yeah, good, now you'll be one of us."

The soon-to-be marrieds pretty much stand around with perpetual smiles on their faces. Some can't wait to be in your shoes while others have issued edicts, planning to the minute: "Oh, now, we have much to do. We're going to wait for a few years. Until we settle in. To be more exact, until March 31, 1979, at 11:33 P.M."

The soon-to-be singles have only one comment to make. Your friend, Caleb, having just told his wife to go to the devil as she threw him out of the back door, has recently moved into a studio apartment, four flights up (no elevator), with a pullman kitchen, a small bathroom where the toilet bowl also doubles as a bathtub, no view, and with 1,700 pictures of his five children taped to the exposed brick wall. He has $325.58 in the bank. She kept the house, the patio, the swim club membership, and both cars, not to mention the five kids, the dog, the dog's leader, and his bowl.

So, when you tell him of your good fortune, he has only two words for you as his bloodshot eyes look into yours: "Happy Birthday."

The singles are a different species. For example, some will be envious of your situation, some couldn't care less, and some will be a combination. Take the girl in the Cacharel blouse, the Valentino slacks, the Ferragamo shoes, and toting a Gucci bag. You think she's going to have a baby slobbering all over that stuff? You think she wants a kid intruding upon her private moments, interfering with her excursions to the Ruptured Duck Pub? Just listen to her:

"Babies? You're kidding. Who needs to be tied down? You don't know what you're in for. I'm having a ball. Good for you, Charles Brown, but not for me. (*Pause*) Oh, by the way, know any single guys in your office?"

And so as we fade into the distance with the phone calls and the questions and the suggestions and the comments arriving from the in-laws, the outlaws, the friends, the neighbors, the guys in the office, the conductors on the train, and the people taking your money at the toll booth, you are now dropped into the position of what to do with all this information.

Recognize that everyone will have his or her two and three cents to put in. Everyone will have a recommendation. Everyone will have a definitive reaction which will be passed on to you. One way or another, everyone is affected by your position, and you would be surprised how this falls into your lap. There may even be unexpected religious problems.

What to do? Let all these people do whatever they want to do, to themselves, that is. Let them enjoy or not enjoy your news. Let them spin themselves silly with advice or let them ignore you completely. As cold-hearted as it sounds, if you listened to each of them, you would not even have time to brush your teeth; you would wind up on the funny farm. These people will offer you enough contradictions to start another political party.

You don't believe me? You think I'm kidding you? Try this one on for size:

"So, who are you using?"

Finding an Obstetrician
"Doctor, Doctor, Who's Got the Doctor?"

Finding an obstetrician to deliver your child is no easy task. First of all, let's understand one thing. To the other sex, obstetricians and gynecologists are important people. Most women have what is known as a gynecologist.

According to Webster, a gynecologist is a "physician specializing in gynecology." Clear? Gynecology? Webster says that it is a "branch of medical science containing physicians specializing in being gynecologists." Clearer now?

Don't listen to him. A gynecologist takes care of the female's reproductive system. The gynecologist is also the chief dispenser of birth control pills and the fitter of all those devices known as diaphragms, IUDs, and the like.

An obstetrician? According to Webster, an obstetrician is a "physician specializing in . . ." You know already what Webster says. An obstetrician, anyway you belabor it, delivers babies.

It should be immediately noted that although most obstetricians do quite a lot of gynecological work, an equal number of gynecologists (especially in the major urban areas) do little obstetrical work. This is because of the high degree of specialization accorded each field. The ones that do both are termed OB–GYN Men. (Yes, there is a chauvinistic attitude.)

As I said before, these doctors are extremely important to the ladies and they should be. The problem we men have is in trying to figure out what all the hoopla is about. For example, I get a sore throat. If it doesn't wash away with three cans of Pabst's, I call Dr. Cavallo.

"Doctor, I got this sore throat. What should I do?"

"Three cans of Miller's."

"Aha, knew I had the wrong brand."

Or, suppose I get a bruised left knee from trying to intercept a ten-year-old's pass to his nine-year-old friend. I call the goodly doctor.

"I got a bruised left knee."

"Still trying to play kids' games, eh, Jack?"

"Uhhhh."

"Okay, here's what to do." And he prescribes the simplest and most logical remedy over the phone: "Take a glass of Dole's pineapple juice, one aspirin, turn on *Bowling for Dollars* and forget about it."

The same applies to my dealings with dentists, dermatologists, opticians, and barbers.

In short, men generally don't go that crazy over doctors nor do we shop that much for them. In fact, when it comes to the medical profession, men don't go shopping at all. Just give us a name we can trust and point us in the right direction.

With women, though, the situation is quite different and understandably so.

"I don't like Doctor Summers."

"Why?"

"He has cold hands."

"I don't like Doctor Tomita."

"Why?"

"He's too Jewish."

"I don't like Doctor Gluckstern."

"Why?"

"He's not Jewish enough."

19

Don't misinterpret. The area these doctors specialize in is an extraordinarily difficult one. First, they are dealing with a physical part of a woman's body which is closest in resemblance to the underground plumbing of Paris. Second, it would be an understatement to say that the area is a highly personal one.

Now, when you start the journey toward selecting an obstetrician (and remember, it's your baby too and I assume you want to know who exactly is to handle your child), the first thing you will probably encounter is Resistance. It comes in many forms. For example, your mother-in-law may try to sell you on Doctor Hornblower. Why? Because he delivered your wife and all twelve of her nieces and nephews. My mother-in-law suggests that we "keep it in the family."

"But, Mom, Doctor Hornblower is ninety years old."

"No matter, he's good. Look, he's got all that experience and you know what the good book says . . ."

"But he can't see and he totters when he walks."

"He has a cane and he doesn't have to see. He knows everything by heart."

Don't laugh. What about *your* mother, wise guy? She insists on Doctor Moss.

"Yes, Mother, I know he's good. Yes, the hospital is certainly an outstanding one. Yes, I know he teaches advanced obstetrics at the university. But, Mother, listen to me. Stop crying, will you Mother? I would love for us to use Doctor Moss, but, Mother, you see, you live in Philadelphia, right? Yes, I know. But, you see, we live in Houston."

Well, what if the recommended doctor *does* live in your town? All right then, let your wife ask her hairdresser, who thinks she knows for sure what you need.

"My doctor is the best. He can deliver with one hand tied behind his back."

Just what you need for your first child. Or,

"My doctor is even better. He does seventy-three deliveries in one week."

Perfect. You can be number seventy-four, squeezed between 9:05 and 9:07 A.M.

To reiterate, it is not easy obtaining a doctor. There are, though, competent ways to choose one.

1. Ask around. I don't mean from those on the preceding pages. Question people who have *recently* given birth and whose opinions you respect. I emphasize "recently." This way, you should get up-to-date information. Obtain facts about their doctors. Where is the office? Does he have other doctors covering for him when he is away? What hospitals is he connected with? You see, many doctors are affiliated with a number of hospitals. You could even select the hospital first and then pick the doctor. (Incidentally, I use the word "he" to represent women doctors, too.)

2. Call the medical society in your area for advice.

3. Check the doctor's credentials in the medical directory found in most libraries or write to the American Medical Association for further information. There is usually a listing in the telephone book.

4. The most important one. Meet the doctor. It is essential that both you and the mother-to-be have a good feeling about him (or her). Above all, ask questions. Don't be afraid of the questions, no matter how silly or unimportant they may appear. You're not an expert in this field. You're not expected to know the answers. Ask, ask, ask. You're paying for it anyway.

What am I talking about? Try these:

What's the doctor's policy on husbands being in the labor and delivery rooms? I'm not kidding. Many people are interested in natural childbirth, and an integral part of that method is the involvement and presence of the male. Therefore, it is necessary that you know the doctor's feelings about this as well as the hospital's policy. Get it settled right at the beginning. You'll be quite miffed at delivery time if someone puts up that Husbands Keep Out sign.

What's the doctor's policy on the use of drugs? This is a very difficult area and even though you are not expected to be a chemist or pharmacologist, you should have an understanding as to whether or not your doctor believes in a liberal or conservative use of drugs. Remember, it's the mother's blood which feeds the baby.

What's the policy of the hospital on rooming-in privileges? In other words, does the baby have to be in a nursery at all times or can it be with the mother for as long as she likes? Some hospitals have changed their methods of delivery dramatically. For example, Memorial Hospital in Phoenix, Arizona, now has what is termed a "Birthing Room" where relatives and friends of the prospective parents can watch the birth. The accommodations contain a living room complete with a sofa, chairs, and a television set, plus a separate bedroom. There is a curtain between the two rooms. Thus, if the parties agree, observers (such as family and friends) can be present *in the bedroom* for the actual delivery.

How often does the doctor want to see you? Yes, I said "you." If you're to be a part of this entire process, then you should have an open line to the doctor at all times and he or she should be able to speak with you whenever necessary. Does the doctor believe in this kind of open-door policy?

Watch what the obstetrician says, and the way it is said. You don't want lazy answers to serious questions. Also, check the doctor's sense of humor. One expectant father told me that it was that point which more than anything else sold him on the doctor.

"We went into his office, he introduced himself and I said right off the bat, 'Look, I don't know anything about babies and you better know it now because I don't know what help I can give.' He just looked at me and laughed. I liked him immediately. He was very calm and could speak on a one-to-one level. He never talked down to me and I liked that. He made me feel very comfortable."

You should also be aware of the fact that an obstetrician sees the woman at least once a month during the first seven months of pregnancy (sometimes more, depending on whether or not there are any complications), but during the last six weeks there may be weekly visits. Also, after the delivery, she will have a checkup at the six-week mark.

So many visits, you say? What's this going to cost? The financial factor in having a baby is a rather distasteful subject to most men. For ease of understanding, let's break this down into doctor and hospital costs.

Most obstetricians work on either an inclusive-fee arrangement or a per-visit charge. It means what it says. One fee for everything, or separate fees for each service. Try to arrange for an all-inclusive fee. It's generally cheaper in the long run. This way, she can see the doctor whenever she feels it necessary; conversely, he can see her at any time without the strain of a per-visit charge sitting over your head. Of course, use your head too. If a per-visit fee is $15 and he expects to see her ten times, plus an additional $250 to deliver the baby, then you might consider that arrangement over a $750 all-inclusive charge.

The actual cost of an obstetrician varies. For example, in New York City it ranges from $600 to $1,000, sometimes a bit less and sometimes considerably more. The fee depends on your area, but New York City can be used as somewhat of a barometer: it's the most expensive place in the country to have a baby.

With respect to hospitals, let's again turn to New York City. At last count, the cost of a semi-private room in a voluntary hospital averaged $160 a day. For a private room, it is $225 a day. The nursery runs on the average of $70 a day. For labor and delivery rooms, figure another $200. Okay now, add all these figures up. Four days in a semi-private room will run you a minimum of $1,100. Incidentally, you will also have to ante up around $700 as a down payment. Some hospitals require this amount as much as 5 months before admission. As I said before, this is the New York area. Los Angeles and San Francisco run about the same while cities such as Philadelphia, Seattle, Phoenix, and New Orleans are two-thirds of the above costs. The prices will dip even more outside the major urban centers.

Why are costs for medical care so high? For obstetricians, the malpractice insurance rates have been a deciding factor, while for hospitals it has been an ever-spiraling escalation of wages and supplies, plus the intricacies of greater technical facilities.

Insofar as insurance is concerned, it is speculated that an insurance plan will pay the difference between the $700 I mentioned above and the final bill of some $1,100 to $1,200 on the hospital . . . if you're lucky. It may also pick up $100 on the obstetrician's bill. This all depends, of course, on your particular insurance plan and your area. It is vitally important then that you check your own policy carefully. There is great variance around the country.

Insurance coverage for maternity is not all that good anyway. Apparently, the insurance people like to pay for the abnormal, not the normal. Thus, if there were complications of a serious nature, then the insurance company would step in and pick up most of the tab. It's a shame that something as natural and as positive as birth should be treated in the shabby manner it is.

In the July 1977, issue of *Consumer Reports* magazine, there is an article regarding a California couple who figured out a bill of $2,000 for the obstetrician and a four-and-one-half day hospital stay. But what the couple found especially interesting was that in another magazine, a major medical insurance company had taken out an ad wherein they talked about the increase in obstetrical costs and asked that its members join with them in keeping "a baby's million dollar smile from turning into a bill just as big." When the couple called that insurance company to find out how much of their $2,000 would be covered, they were told that the costs of normal childbirth above $150 are excluded. That's right, EXcluded!

So, when you total all the costs, you will be talking in terms of at least a $1,500 to $2,000 out-of-pocket expense just to bring that baby into the world and into your house. There is certainly nothing wrong with discussing all these fees and costs with the recommended doctor. In fact, such a discussion is encouraged.

There are some doctors and some hospitals you may not be able to afford. If you can't cut it with such fees, there are various clinical programs around which you might want to explore. For instance, turning again to New York, one hospital has a special package deal: For under $500, you get 4 days in a semi-private room and use of the nursery and the delivery room. It even includes delivery of the baby by a staff resident or midwife. In fact, there are some clinical arrangements which cover prenatal and postpartum care. New maternity facilities such as the one just mentioned are cropping up all around the country and you need only to seek them out.

To reemphasize what has been said in the preceding pages, don't hesitate to question the doctor in detail. Notwithstanding the fact that the mother-to-be may be enamored of a particular obstetrician, it is still your duty as the father-to-be to see his office, to make sure what his fee includes, to check out his credentials, and to be satisfied that you will be getting what you need.

Remember what we discussed earlier on your fears and concerns? The obstetrician is one of the persons who can furnish you with some of the solutions to these problems. If he is worth his salt, he has been around the block before on what is important in a prospective father's mind. Although he may be her doctor, technically, he can certainly be of immeasurable value and comfort to you. One other factor. Be open when choosing an obstetrician. Have a flexible mind. You know the adage, you can't really tell a book by its cover? The same applies here. Sometimes, looks are deceiving.

In our case, we selected one through the recommendation of a number of people we respected: friends, other physicians. We also checked out the doctor's credentials at the library. They were quite good. Nancy said his telephone voice was most soothing and she promptly set up an appointment for us to meet him.

His office was painted in a funny shade of green. Five Keane paintings hung on the walls. Magazines were neatly stacked in one corner. There were comfortable easy chairs and plenty of them.

The doctor was tall, slim, youthful. I would say early forties. He had gray eyes, thinning hair, and a healthy complexion. He wore a white gown, a red knit tie, and no jewelry except for one of those fancy chronometers. In short, he was normal—for a doctor—and I liked him instantly. He also had a sense of humor, for he kept humming a melody—I think it was the theme from *Rosemary's Baby*.

Well, you can't have everything, can you?

Incidentally, if you forgot to ask the doctor at that first visit, you may want to know what your kid looks like at this stage of the game, so . . .

A Special Report from the Inside—Second Month

The baby-to-be is called an embryo or fetus. It is about an inch in length. Certain external organs are present but in a rather primitive form. The arms have cuplike hands with the start of fingers and thumbs. The legs have tiny bumps (buds, as they are called) from which the knees, ankles, and toes will eventually develop.

There is a face being formed: eyes, ears, nose, mouth, but actually this is more of an outline than any definitive shape. Some of the internal organs are beginning to function. For example, the liver is producing blood and the kidneys are starting to excrete waste products.

During this period, the embryo floats about in a sac filled with fluid. This fluid recycles those waste products through the mechanism of the mother's body. The sac itself is connected to the placenta, which in turn is attached to the wall of the uterus by the umbilical cord. Air and food come to the embryo by way of this cord.

You may wonder why it's important for you to know what's going on inside the woman. For one reason, it will help you to understand what is going on with the woman herself. Remember, this book is geared to your survival and what happens to her has a direct effect on you.

More importantly, don't forget that you are to be a father soon and you'll find it much easier all the way around, both during and after pregnancy, to have some relevant information at your fingertips. Would Tom Seaver ever think of just trooping off to the mound without a pretty good knowledge of each batter he is to face? By the same token, you should have as much information at your side as is possible.

Now, more about all those unanswered questions. Here's another way you can find some of the answers.

What to Read
"To Read or Not to Read"

Along with everything else, there will be a wealth of reading material flying your way: books, magazines, newspapers, pamphlets. You name it; somehow you'll see it. Nearly every author, publisher, doctor, mother, and mother-in-law has contemplated or produced a book on pregnancy. One of the reasons this book was written was precisely that fact. There had been too, too much on the mother-to-be and not enough about and for the father-to-be.

One factor remains constant. There will always be room for more books about babies and parents and there will always be people writing them and people reading them. Everyone has his or her own experience to share and you would be surprised at how many "new" things turn up, which are really "old" things; that is, similar sets of facts.

That's the key right there. Most books on the subject generally say the same thing. If you look at the chapter headings in any number of them, you will find an identical format. There will be a thorough course on what happens to the body during the first few weeks of pregnancy; in fact, almost every book worth its dust jacket contains graphics, diagrams, and charts tracing how the embryo grows into a baby, depicting in vivid detail what transpires at the end of each month.

Don't get me wrong. Most of the books out today are good ones. Some, of course, are better than others. But by and large it takes a combination of books, a chapter from that one and a chapter from that one to make a complete, sensible approach to this entire matter. I know that there are those who say a little knowledge can be dangerous. True, to a certain extent, but a little knowledge may also help answer your unanswered questions.

Originally, I thought it was a bit much to rely on books. What could I learn that I really needed to? The woman of my house, however, thought differently.

She bought every one imaginable, until the bookcase groaned under the sheer weight of all this information. Why? My wife, bless her 5'2" heart, is a literary maven. This does not mean that she is a flaming, dyed-in-the-Orlon intellectual. It does mean, though, that she accumulates every book available on a given subject once she zeroes in on it.

So, when the clinic waved the green flag and the musically inclined doctor issued a confirmation, she began reaching into the depths of all her publishing sources (she was director of advertising, publicity, and promotion at a major publishing company). What resulted was a roundup of virtually every book about pregnancy ever written. After all, she was now past thirty; this was her first child and she intended to do it right from the beginning.

Needless to say, the books began piling up in every corner of our apartment. Walk into the bathroom and there were at least seventy-five pieces of reading material, enough for a minimum of 3,000 visits. Go into the kitchen for some Raisin Bran and you would discover another seventy-five. You could polish off Kellogg's production of Raisin Bran for a year without even denting the kitchen's reading material. Of course, by doing so, you would probably be able to get through the bathroom supply that much faster.

One thing you should keep in mind. A lot of books are the experiences of other women. Now, this may not really be of particular interest to you, unless you are willing to empathize with tales of recurring heartburn. What's the real importance to you in knowing that Ellen has this nauseous feeling after she eats coconuts or Jill has a ringing in her ears whenever she brushes with Gleem? Do you really need to know all this?

But remember one thing: It is still your child and as long as that lady over there is going to be feeding it and walking with it and taking care of it for the next nine months (and thereafter), you should understand something (no matter how meager) about what is going on in her body. As my mother would say, "It wouldn't hurt."

The books will tell you many things, a lot of which, as I said before, are not really geared to you. Nevertheless, after seeing what was brought into my house, I can make certain evaluations of which books might prove the most beneficial, both during the pregnancy and after the baby arrives.

At this stage, I would particualrly recommend the following:

Pregnancy, Birth and Family Planning, by Dr. Alan G. Guttmacher. This is one of the finest books ever written on the subject. It is published by Viking Press (a paperback edition is published by New American Library) and is a 350-page work covering a multitude of areas from conception to twin births. The author, a distinguished physician, has been called the elder statesman on a wide range of social issues, from sterilization to sexual freedom.

For a more psychological approach, you might want to read *The Natural Way to Raise a Healthy Child*, by Hiag Akmakjian, published by Praeger. Dr. Akmakjian is a psychoanalyst and his major thesis is that the key to the baby's (and eventually the adult's) mental health is the dependable emotional availability of the parents. Dr. Akmakjian takes the view that not just children but parents too have rights.

Finally, how about something just for her? I would recommend one which stands head and shoulders above the others of its kind. It is called *Birth*, by Caterine Milinaire, and is published by Harmony Books. As the jacket says, "*Birth* is a labor of love from many mothers and fathers to all expectant parents." It covers, among other things, the development of the embryo, body care, methods of childbirth, experiences by men and women, infant care, and customs around the world. It's a perfect gift for the expectant mother.

As long as we're in the area of advice and information, whether from doctors or books, you should be aware of the many pieces of counsel which will be dropped on you by an assortment of persons. La Rochefoucauld once said, "One gives nothing so liberally as advice." I say, you get what you pay for!

Old Wives' Tales
    "Take it easy."
    "Don't take it easy."
    "Jogging is good for you."
    "Jogging is bad for you."

"Think good thoughts."
"Don't think at all."
"Don't read books, listen to your doctor."
"Don't listen to your doctor, listen to your mother."
"Don't listen to your mother, listen to your friends."
"Don't listen to your friends, read the books."
"Don't read the books, listen to your . . ."

This is the area in which the greatest number of problems arise. According to our friend Webster, an old wives' tale is a "traditional tale or bit of lore . . . a superstitious notion." The term is derived from certain old wives in Russia ages ago who wanted to pass on to the younger wives the "secrets" of childbirth and child rearing. That was all well and good but these secrets have been expanded upon to such a point that the wives of old Russia have been shunted aside in favor of newer elements of advice.

This latest breed of experts includes:

1. Friends of yours who have never been married, will never marry, and who know nothing about babies except that they are smaller than adults

2. Friends who are married or have been married, and also know nothing about babies, never having had any and never intending to

3. Family and other assorted relatives whose knowledge about babies comes from what they see in the television commercials

4. Friends and family who have had children and who have accumulated all the answers

All these people can be harbingers of misinformation. They are famous for setting up nonsensical rules and regulations. Most of them invented the word "don't" and they use it as a direct negative. They also invented the word "do" and use it as a command negative. For example, *don't do* any exercises. *Do* get out of bed slowly. *Don't* bathe in warm water. *Do* stay away from certain people.

Now, what are the truths? What are the correct answers to some of these edicts?

After checking with a number of doctors, I have come up with a handful of answers to a handful of these orders. Let's take a few of them. Remember, while they concern the woman, they are most useful to your new role as dispeller of myths and keeper of the nitty-gritty truths.

"Don't do any exercises during pregnancy." Why? "It's bad for the growing fetus."

This is nonsense. Although the mother-to-be should always check with her doctor first, exercising, in moderation, is advocated by most of the medical people, unless reasons of health dictate that the woman remain as immobile as possible during the nine-month period. To dispel that old myth, exercise is not harmful. If anything, it is beneficial. And the baby does it too. You know all the movements the baby makes? That is exercising on his/her part.

"Do remember to get out of bed slowly." Reason? "You'll startle the baby."

Would you believe that one? Perhaps you should tap on the tummy and sing a reveille. In any event, quick movements will *not* upset the baby. Remember, your child is protected in a cushioned sac. It is surrounded by the mother's own shock-absorbing system. Have no fear.

"Don't forget that warm tub baths are bad because the water will come inside and drown the baby."

You mean cold tub baths are okay?

"Stay away from people who have more than one child of

33

the same sex because if you don't, you will have a child of the same sex."

This is exactly how it was told to me by my Aunt Ethel. She wagged a finger at the same time. That being so, how can you possibly fault this brand of logic?

"If she sticks out in front, it's a boy. If she's big in the back, it's a girl."

Now wait, let me explain this concept. What it means is that if the woman carries high and pointed, it will be a boy, but if she's carrying low and spread out, you've got a girl on your hands.

There is no sound medical reason for this. The baby's sex is determined at the time of conception and how it grows is really irrelevant. There is nothing, absolutely nothing which supports this high-pointed and low-spread determination. My wife carried high and pointed and you will see what we got at the end of this book.

The same medical response applies to the use of ouija boards, tarot readings, swinging rings, hand signals, and the like. It's all bunk. Oh, there is one exception. The paternal grandfather. If you want to know the sex of your baby, ask him. He has a very high batting average.

"Don't drink liquor while pregnant or else the baby will have too much alcohol in its blood."

This deserves some consideration. Although it is categorized as an old wives' tale, it may very well contain some seeds of truth. Moderation is still the key to everything. Unless there is a health problem, an occasional glass of wine, beer, or scotch cannot possibly hurt either the mother or the baby. In fact, it has been shown that alcohol may aid in digestion. Again, moderation is the password.

"Don't travel by air." Why? "Too much pressure on the baby."

True? Of course not. Flying generally has no effect on the baby. Naturally, I wouldn't suggest you wind up in a plane over the Arctic Circle during the ninth month or decide to take up stunt flying at that time. That's a helluva spot for her to go into labor.

These few bits of advice are only small representations of the scattered thousands upon thousands of mandates, recommendations, helpful hints, and "gospel truths" which have been passed down through the ages. They have been codified, systematized, and classified. However, most of them are generally misguided, misdirected, and misinformed—in other words, dead wrong.

What is the best advice? *Ask your doctor*. He should be running the show. Check some of the more reputable books and most importantly, listen to yourself. You know whether it is wise to involve your wife in a round of jai alai while she's in the seventh month, and you also know whether it is beneficial to her condition to enter her in a chug-a-lug beer contest twice a week.

What can *you* do about all this unasked-for advice? Ignore, Ignore, Ignore.

Of course, that may be tough to do. Undoubtedly, there are those of you who would rather switch than fight. Okay for you, but I have found that one of the best remedies is still the "out-of-focus" method. This maneuver can be used in almost any given situation.

For instance, Aunt Ethel corners you. She looks you squarely in the face and continues listing the do's and don'ts. You stare back at her, nod an occasional "yes" and focus on the tip of her nose. As you concentrate, begin thinking of trying to jump over that nose as in the high jump.

If you concentrate well enough and long enough, you

will envision yourself in red shorts and white Pumas, making a run from somewhere down around the brooch on her neck, up past her mouth, circling the left cheek and then hurdling the bridge of her nose in a perfect Fosbury Flop à la Dwight Stones. Ahhhh!

The best advice, however, is not always the easiest. If you have difficulty in looking at Aunt Ethel's nose, then you must turn to the Tube in the corner. Tune in *The Bionic Woman* while Aunt Ethel continues her sermon. Nod quietly and catch the show out of the corner of your eye. Eventually Aunt Ethel will either leave you alone or leave altogether. And isn't that what you wanted anyway? Of course, when the baby's born, she may not give you a check, but . . .

Mental Effects on You
"I Think I'm Going Out of My Mind."

By now you must have realized that your head is beginning to take on the shape of a dirigible being filled. This is just the beginning. The brain inside is doing mental gymnastics. The reason? Because of all this new and confusing information.

One of the problems you may have at this time is distinguishing between what advice is meant for her, what is meant for you, what is meant for the both of you, and what is not meant for her, you or both. It boils down to what *not* to believe.

Most of what you hear is angled toward the woman so that when all this gets to her, what can you expect? There may be a wide range of emotions, running the gamut from "I'm going crazy" to "You don't love me any more," to "I'm fat and ugly," to "I'm being suffocated."

All true. She is probably experiencing these feelings and lots more. Consider this. Suppose your wife has been working diligently for a number of years building a career and is now making good money. How do you think she's going to feel when all of a sudden she's with child and that career may be coming to an abrupt end?

You can easily come up with your own example. But whatever it is the situation is not a simple one for her unless, of course, you married someone whose idea of a good time is to change a diaper with one hand, feed another kid with the other, and keep a rocker going with her right foot. If that's the case, knock on wood.

Whatever affects the woman will have an effect on you. Try our old friend "fear." This is particularly apparent in a woman who is experiencing her first child. How would you feel with something growing inside you? If you are like me, you'd be wondering how it's supposed to come out. When you really stop and think about it, the whole thing doesn't seem to make much sense anyway, the logistics of it all. It's like trying to force an elephant through a keyhole. This is only one fear, but it may be enough to set off an emotional upheaval.

Okay now, what happens to you while things are happening to her? For the most part, you will be experiencing a tap dance on your headbone. Why? Because your lady's moods will be changing rapidly. One expectant father told me, "She got so damn moody and it showed with everything I did or said. We would argue over nothing—silly things like how good were the leftovers."

During pregnancy, she may not be the same person. She may become two different people. Pregnancy can be a strain on the woman, make no mistake about it. These may be tense times. By her actions, you will become acutely aware of your increased obligations and the fact that she may no longer be focusing that much attention on you. As she becomes more involved with her own body, you may also experience a real loss in her interest toward you. Don't worry. This is only temporary. The proper attitude to maintain during this rather unsettling period is extremely important.

"She would laugh and cry at the same time."

"She was more sensitive. She needed a lot of support."

"Became picky. The weather would affect her."

"Cries easily."

"Talks constantly."

It may not sound like fun, but remember one thing. These nine months are transitory ones. *Your* concern is to keep *your* head together and, of course, there is no better way of starting off on the right foot than at the beginning. In the immortal words of Casey Stengel, "When all around you have lost their heads, you must remember to keep your hat on straight." How can you best do this? How can you keep things on the straight and narrow, not only to help yourself, but to help her as well?

First Rule. Don't read *all* the books written on the subject. They will only tend to confuse you and make you sleepy. Try the few recommended here. For other reading, try mystery stories. It's good escape material. If you stick to the *Playboy/Penthouse* stuff, you are asking for trouble. As you will see in a few more pages, the sex area can be difficult enough without lending it a helping hand.

Second Rule. If you listen to every medical expert, you will get completely befuddled. Stick to your obstetrician or your own therapist if you have one. Don't look for additional medical opinions on every change in her mood. In other words, don't be so defensive.

Third Rule. Keep some distance between you and your mother. She may be a boy's best friend, but if you want to listen for the zillionth time how small you were at birth and how the nurses wrapped you in cotton and put you in an incubator, then you deserve what you get. Mothers are great for baby-sitting, but only for the baby.

It is best not to consider too seriously the advice given so readily by friends during this period. Although they mean well, they might drive you crazy, if you let them. For instance, your friend Otto at the plant: "Herbie, old pal, things are certainly going to change in a few months. I have· only one good tip for you and that is, you *better* earn more money."

That kind of pressure (even if true) you don't need.

Friends are well-meaning and Lord knows you need some, but it's hard to be serious with a buddy who has five kids of his own and who, everytime he sees you, goes into hysterics.

"Oh, wait until you see what's going to happen to you." (Remember that old radio program? "Are they gone? Ooooo, what's going to happen to them.")

Fourth Rule. This is probably the most important one of all. Get your wife to talk about her fears. The key here is to communicate, to get the feelings out on the table where they can be seen and handled. If professional help is needed, then use it. This is no time to harbor hostilities. They will only surface in a detrimental way later.

A well-known and highly respected obstetrician in New York City says, "The women do need more attention at this time and the men should be prepared to be more sensitive and understanding. Couples should be supportive of each other." These are the fundamental points to remember: sensitivity, understanding, support.

During this nine-month period and particularly when you reach the last few months, some women may get irrational. They may go through valleys and peaks and, as a result, you can easily get sucked into a nonsensical babbling contest:

"You don't love me."

"Of course I do."

"You don't show it."

"How?"

"You can buy me that."

"Buy you that?"

"Yes."

"How can I do that?"

"See, you don't love me."

"Of course I do, but how can I buy you that? You're not making any sense."

"You're saying I'm crazy?"

"No, no. But how can I buy you . . . ?" as you gaze up the side of the Empire State Building.

Sensitivity, understanding, support.

So, who really needs it?

Sex and You: Part 1

Larry and Ivy have just turned out the light. She gives a little moan, a sigh. He hears it. His eyes open wide.

He hears another sound, a kind of "ohh" followed by an "ahh." He rolls to his left and settles one hand on a breast.

She arches her back ever so slightly and turns toward him. He now arches his back, ever so slightly, and a bit more. Sex will never be better, he hears himself saying. It is sunk deep within him, pounded there by Barry, the office manager, Fred, the mailman, Charlie, the shoeshine guy, and Leonard, the ten-year-old who sells lemonade on the corner.

He snuggles to her, plants his lips against her cheek and

drills his nose into a dimple. Another moan, followed by another sigh, and then the "ohh" and the "ahh." They all seem to blend.

She has never made these sounds before, he thinks. Obviously, this pregnancy must be agreeing with her. Such an "ohh" and such an "ahh." Hooray, the whole wide world is right. Sex will never be better.

He moves his hand from her breast and slides it down to her navel and begins to make small circles on top of the pubic bone. She arches even more and he buries his mouth into her dimple. His dong is already in the dinging position. He closes his eyes. He hears the moaning and the sighing and the "ohhing" and the "ahhing" and then a *Whish!*

His eyes open. No, it couldn't be. It couldn't possibly be. He waits a moment. Her eyes are closed. She looks as though she might have stopped breathing. He decides to continue. Onward with the pressing and the throbbing and the arching.

She resumes her moaning and sighing and "ohhing" and "ahhing" and "ooing" (something new has been added) and then her body tightens once again: *Whish!*

He lifts his face from her dimple.

"Ivy, I was wondering . . . uhhhh."

He hears his name murmured.

"Larry?"

"Yes, Ivy."

"I don't think, Larry, this is the time, Larry."

There is a pause. In the past, that would have been enough to cool him off quickly. This time he decides to confront the situation headlong. Four years on the couch taught him that.

"Could you explain, Ivy? All that moaning and sighing and ohhing and ahhing."

41

"And ooing."

"Yeah, that too."

"Oh, Larry, it isn't you. It's this . . ." And she points to her middle.

Poor Larry, as was poor Barry and poor Fred and poor Charlie and poor Leonard. All revved up and nowhere to go. And all they can hear are those familiar words: "I have gas." *Whish*.

The problem of sex and what can be done about it is not a laughing matter. There are some who would say don't let it get to you. A very simple approach, but too simple. During this initial one-third of the pregnancy term, you may be dealing with *her* nausea, gas, morning sickness, evening sickness, and general guilt, as well as *your* feeling of virility, happiness, and shock. The result? Sex may not come that easily.

Although your first impression is that she is already pregnant and, therefore, what harm can you do, the doctor may quickly point out, "Aha, watch yourself because the first three months are important to determine if it will hold."

The doctor is referring to the fetus. At this stage, it is probably the size of a walnut, attached to the uterine wall, and it is during this period that the bulk of miscarriages occur. The mother-to-be has probably gained about five pounds and the uterus has already pushed up into the abdominal cavity; in fact, it has reached halfway to the navel. In short, everything is in a rather tenuous state and, accordingly, some caution must be exercised.

Now, don't get me wrong. The caution is chiefly administered by the lady. She has to make sure she doesn't rush pell-mell into a department store's revolving doors, or get jostled too much while trying to score two points on the roller derby track. She's the one who has to be extra careful, especially if there is any history of miscarriages.

All right then, what does this mean for you? It means that sex can continue, but saner measures have to be enacted. Tenderness has now got to govern your actions. Don't forget that this may be one of the few times she can enjoy sex without worrying about becoming pregnant, but even with that concern put to bed, discretion in the way you do things is of the utmost importance.

Although the introduction of new positions is not needed until the middle months of pregnancy, you should, however, shelve your usual pre-pregnancy tactics. No more rape attacks, no more bouncing, no more contorted positions, no more devices or gimmicks.

There is, though, one bright spot among all those negatives, a rose among the thorns. Her bosom will expand. By this time the breasts are extremely sensitive to the touch. Thus, the squeezing-pulling-pushing routine you previously followed is no longer effective. But (and this is the crux of it), during pregnancy it is essential for the woman to toughen her nipples, especially if she wants to breast-feed. Statistics show that more and more women are breast-feeding; therefore, tough nipples are the Order of the Day.

Why? Because during the first couple of weeks of nursing sore and cracked nipples can become an obvious problem.

How does this help you? Well, there are a few ways women can toughen their nipples during pregnancy:

1. There are simple exercises.
2. There are certain creams.
3. There is stimulation.

That last one is where you come in. A number of doctors advocate the help of the male to stimulate the breasts manually and *orally*. Enough said?

Your New Physical Problems

With the shifting characteristics of sex comes another problem. You will undoubtedly see an enormous change in what your wife looks like. At first, it will not be too noticeable. There may be certain symptoms as previously mentioned: morning nausea, gas, heartburn. But, later on some symptoms may manifest themselves into an array of interesting conditions: constipation, varicose veins, nasal congestion, backache, insomnia, faintness, skin rashes, itchy skin, frequent urination.

Of course, at her fingertips will be all the remedies the modern world has produced: Tums, Ex-Lax, Maalox, Kaopectate, Desitin, Intensive Care Lotion, Neo-Synephrine, Tylenol—all lined up in the medicine cabinet.

Her body will start expanding, usually by the end of the third month. She may even sport a line down the middle of her abdomen. Her umbilicus may be swollen.

However, the gist of this section is not what is happening to her. Whatever you need to know about the physical changes in her body can easily be obtained by taking a peek at the many books on the market. No, we are talking about you.

One morning I noticed a little bump on the thumb knuckle of my left hand. By the afternoon the bump spread out like a water blister, except that it wasn't soft like a water blister. It was hard and sprouting upward like a pimple. Except that it wasn't a pimple, either. The whole thing was maybe an eighth of an inch by an eighth of an inch, that being the perfect size and shape for a wart and which, according to the kindly Dr. Silvers, was exactly what it was. I have always had clean, pure, smooth skin without a blemish or wart or pockmark, other than occasional and quite discriminatory freckles. So, where did this wart come from? Nerves? A virus? What?

That's wart number one. I also have wart number two on my right index finger and wart number three on my left pinky finger. That's not all. I'm picking up everything from earlobe rashes to jock itch.

That, my friends, may be the first physical change. Unfortunately, it is taking place in you. One expectant father commiserated with me. "I'm getting the same kind of reactions except my face is breaking out in all kinds of pimples. I now have to use Clearasil—Clearasil, would you believe it? And I'm thirty-six years old. I guess this pregnancy is getting to me more than I realize."

As the pregnancy picks up steam, there will be a number of other, different physical changes which will occur. Note that word "different." You will witness unsettling changes in your well-being aside from just obtaining skin problems.

You will observe before too long that your wife's body temperature fluctuates a great deal and it's never in tune with what's going on outside. For example, in the summertime the air conditioner will undergo a heavy workout. I don't mean it will be running constantly. No. Instead, it will be changed more often than a newborn.

It's 10 P.M. 90 degrees out. You're roasting. She turns the dial from "High Cool" to "Low Cool."

It's 2 A.M. It's dropped to 65 degrees *outside*. The dial has now been changed from "Low Cool" to "Super Cool." You think you're in the tundra.

6 A.M. The hot sun is beginning to peek in. You feel as though you are sleeping on a 100-degree sidewalk getting ready to be turned over lightly. She moves the dial to the "Off" position.

In the winter, the heating element is operated in much

The Expectant Father's Survival Kit

the same way. There is not a whole lot you can do about this unless you choose to live in a separate room during the nine-month period.

We're not finished. You will be exposed to other subtle changes in your physical appearance. Yes, I reiterate the "your." This generally comes under the heading of "Sloppiness."

If you haven't been a pigpen up to now, you will certainly become one by the time this pregnancy is over. How? Well, you know the holes in your socks? They will begin to grow in proportion to the growth of her stomach. They get larger as she gets larger. The same concept applies equally to your shirts. You will find that the ring around your collar has now extended to include your shoulders. Your suits will look as if Bruno Sammartino had slept in them. Instead of carrying a neatly folded handkerchief in your back pocket, you will sport folded Charmin.

In brief, you may have to use everything in your power to keep whatever is left of your ship in top running condition, or for that matter, in any condition.

Don't worry about her. She will be perfectly fine. She may find it difficult arising from a chair or bed, but she will explain to you in dulcet tones that there really is no need for her to get up for a glass of milk or to turn the tub water on, not when you, healthy you, are standing at the ready.

Additionally, you will find her sleeping more. This is known as conserving one's energy—hers. The problem is that the conservation policy seems to be in effect only while you are at home. She finds it an enormous chore to rise on a Saturday morning and make breakfast. Actually, she finds it a chore to do most anything. Now, don't get me wrong. She may not be lazy. She's just going through a rather awkward and difficult time.

46

Then, too, in the evening it's amazing how much she can sleep: right at the dinner table, after she insists she wants to do the dishes. "I think I'll take a short nap before I start." Thunk! The head drops forward. She is gone for the night.

You do have some outs here. First of all, get her mind off being tired. How? One smart way is to keep her occupied. This means if she's working, she should stay at it. My wife worked until the last month. My next-door neighbor went at it until the week she delivered. If your wife is not already working, find her something to do. Painting the house is one suggestion.

Notwithstanding the above, once that head hits the table and she is in never-never land, you have your choice: You can either hire a housemaid to do the dishes and the cooking, or you can do it all yourself. Before you make that decision, let me lay a few more goodies on you.

It costs money to hire help and money may be a problem inasmuch as there are a good many costs popping in from a number of unexpected sources. For example, during this period it is important that the mother-to-be visit a dentist. Pregnancy has a tendency to soften the gums and extract calcium from the teeth. Accordingly, a pregnant woman is more susceptible to gum problems and tooth decay.

How does this affect you? In the pocketbook. Be prepared for this expensive item before you decide to hire someone to make soft-boiled eggs at $10 an hour. You can always learn to boil water but you can't always learn to treat pyorrhea.

You will also probably experience a change in your weight. I kid you not. Expect either to lose ten to fifteen pounds without blinking an eyelid, or gain an equal amount in an equal period of time. Again, I am not talking about her; it's you.

47

Don't worry about her. She will do very nicely indeed. She will be infused with a wide array of vitamins, plenty of milk, and all the proper foods. She will become the poster girl for the National Nutrition Council. But you, aha! You will gain weight as you try to empathize with your wife's expanding girth. "I now have someone to eat with. It's sympathy pains. My diet went kaput."

Or, you will soon notice that where her abdomen begins to bulge, yours will begin to recede. You should without any trouble flatten to about nothing. The cause? Simple. She is not cooking like she used to and what she is now cooking is hardly meat 'n taters and homemade peach pie with chocolate chip ice cream. Her eating habits will become more erratic. And you? Ten to fifteen pounds guaranteed. Either way.

Her Nutrition and Your Stomach

When we talk about nutrition in the expectant mother, we are really talking about what she can and cannot eat and what she can and cannot drink and, consequently, what you can and cannot eat and can and cannot drink. This primarily means that she will probably be consuming certain kinds of foods, commonly known as "everything good."

The first thing you will notice is that she will begin to gorge herself daily with obscene-looking pink pills. These pink pills, which are the size of infant torpedoes, have many names. Each pharmaceutical company has its own brand name, but the most common one used today is made by Mead Johnson, the same people who gave us Metrecal. It is called Natalins. A very good handle indeed. Natalins is a multivitamin and multimineral supplement for, and catch this from the label, "pregnant and lactating women." Lactating means secreting milk. Therefore, if she will be breast-feeding you will continue to smell these pills around the house even after the pregnancy is over. This vitamin contains an incredible army of ingredients: ten vitamins, four minerals, and enough other things to make you wonder why each pill isn't the size of an ICBM.

You would normally think this was enough. I would normally think this was enough. Who wouldn't think this was enough? Not enough. Certainly not all that can be done. Pregnant women have one thing in common: food, vitamins, and minerals, in whatever form and in whatever way they come.

Coupled with the nutritional value of these pink pills, you will be a first-hand observer to the female's craving for other good commodities. The pickles and ice cream routine has gone the way of the old Tom Mix westerns. If you want to hear about such combinations at three in the morning, then you had better tune in to one of those Cary Grant movies on the *Late, Late Show*. It will not be applicable today. In fact, whether pregnant or not, how many women, how many people, kids, even stray dogs, will consume a jar of Heinz' sweet gherkins and a carton of Breyer's all-natural vanilla at the same sitting—or at any sitting?

What will more likely happen is that she will begin to seek out advice on her own as to what is and what is not the best thing to eat. Pregnant women will go the way of the books, too, and what is contained in them, meaning, "Eat those things which are going to be good not only for you, but also for the baby."

If she's been reading all the books she bought, she's probably gone nuts about nutrition. Don't question it. It will help you both feel and look better. There is certainly nothing wrong with consuming healthful foods. However, there is a question of degree. Does she go overboard? If so, how far?

Quarts and quarts of Light 'n Lively every day? Lettuce

and wheat germ sandwiches in your lunch box? Tuna and bean sprouts? Special K, prunes, and skim milk for breakfast, a health salad for lunch washed down by canned apricots, and for dinner one bite-sized piece of baked chicken with a tomato and some eggplant? See what I mean?

The problem surrounding this is that her eating habits, as odd as they may seem, do vary from week to week, from day to day, from minute to minute. They are not constant, so that when they do fluctuate, you may be caught right smack in the middle of what appears to be inconsistent insanity.

To explain. My wife began eating in different phases—that is, her meals corresponded to her moods on any given day. For one month straight, she must have eaten at least 753 bananas each day. Maybe I'm exaggerating a little, but the place certainly smelled as if a monkey had moved in. Naturally, the first question I had was what effect such a large dosage would have on her and the offspring. I got part of my answer on a recent visit to the Bronx Zoo where she was whistled at by every gorilla, chimpanzee, and orangutan.

For another month, she gave up on the bananas and started in on milk shakes. Now, as every woman past the age of eight will tell you, milk shakes are out-of-bounds. They will put weight on anyone, even a ninety-eight-pounder who gets sand kicked in her face. It's that slushy combination of milk, ice cream, and syrup which will do you in.

But her answer? "I'm fat anyway."

Other men I have spoken to witnessed similar actions in their spouses:

"She had a penchant for cookies. All kinds: Oreos, chocolate chips, Mallomars, even zwieback."

"She got crazy over sunflower seeds. I walked in them. I slept with them. I sat on them. Crack, crack, crack."

"I'm on the Pennsylvania Turnpike at 7 A.M. It's the dead of winter. It's twenty-nine miles to the nearest exit and thirty-one miles to Howard Johnson's. She screams at me, 'If I don't have a vanilla ice cream cone with chocolate sprinkles right now, I'll die.' "

One thing you might want to keep in mind. She may not necessarily be craving for food alone. An uncontrollable eating pattern may be a sign of a great yearning for affection. She may be feeling that you do not love her as she is no longer attractive. Remember, much of the pregnant woman's sense of ugliness is psychological. However, most of the men I have talked with couldn't understand this reaction. "I think she's her prettiest when pregnant. There's a glow about her. I loved it."

If this is what you feel about her, then you should communicate this feeling to her.

You will also find that various publications will dictate how she should take care of herself. This is echoed in the women's magazines at least once every two months when they publish long and involved lists of what certain foods contain in the way of vitamins and minerals and calories. It can get out of hand. By the third month in our house, I couldn't even find the refrigerator. It was covered from stem to stern with lists: white lists, purple lists, striped lists, flowered lists, all centered around the Food Problem.

What food problem, you ask? Apparently, *we* are not eating properly. Would you believe that a recent dinner consisted of beef liver, broccoli, cantaloupe, and tomato juice? Why? Because, according to the polka-dotted list, they were considered all-star foods.

You see, this list categorizes foods. Some become all stars

and some become minor leaguers, or worse. (The play-up to men is quite obvious.) According to the anonymous authors of this list, each dish should contain at least a certain number of points and a good food would contain a minimum of 50 points.

They feel that a 50-point consumption per dish per meal per day is going great. Sort of like having a 50-point basketball average. Now, that's an all star.

So, for last night's dinner, there was two ounces of beef liver containing 172 points, three-and-one-third ounces of broccoli containing 116 points, a quarter of a cantaloupe for 99 points, and eight ounces of tomato juice sliding in at 52 points. Any way you eat it, they come out to a pretty good total and you will have broken Wilt Chamberlain's one-game record at that sitting. Think of it: liver, broccoli, cantaloupe, and tomato juice. Could you really? Okay, occasionally, but . . .

Remember those days of reaching into the old fridge for a late-night snack of Morton's coconut cream pie? Now, it's nowhere to be found. Why? Because a slab of it is minus 62 points. Minus, no less. A can of Coke? No good. Minus 92 points. Even plain Jello-O. A minus 45. (Alpo dog food, however, is *plus* 10.) What are these foods called? Junk foods. Somebody, somewhere termed them junk foods.

They all have the unique property of bearing minus signs. That means for each Milky Way you ate, you had to pay back 34 points. Nowadays, every new kitchen becomes equipped with a calculator, a scale, and a timetable.

In any event, our refrigerator, including the adjacent walls, overflowed with lists of such all-star foods and of such junk foods. There is no question but that this makes for fascinating reading. It also serves to blunt your appetite each time you start for your nightly raid. As long as the list says chocolate marshmallows are a junk food, you will not find a chocolate marshmallow in the house. Take a gander at what's in the refrigerator: no beer, no Coke; only Tab and milk. Look in the cupboard: no Yankee Doodles, no Beefaroni; only cans of Bumble Bee. Try the breadbox: no French bread, no Oreos; only a green-looking protein loaf.

You think it's funny watching *Police Woman* while sucking on carrot sticks?

Along with the foods represented on these lists, your house will also be inundated with health foods. At last count, we had more millers bran, wheat germ, sunflower seeds, and sprouted mung beans than the nearby emporium which stocks these items. We're now their supplier.

The problem, of course, gets compounded. Ever finish a delightful, nutritious meal of broiled cod, cooked squash, kale, and more tomato juice and then go to a movie like *Tom Jones?*

One other thought must be kept in mind when you venture into the food arena. A lot of the foods which she brings into the house could be aphrodisiacs. No fooling.

An aphrodisiac usually ignites the sexual desire. This may be the last thing you need at this point, but it may be the first thing for you to consider. For example, spinach is considered an aphrodisiac *par excellence*. It is also rated 104 on the all-star food scale. The results of eating such a food can, of course, be maddening. Not only does it enhance your sexual vigor, but it does so by making you even healthier. Now you have the answer to Popeye's success. He was just turned on too much.

So, when you have certain foods foisted upon you, consider what they really do to you. Watch out for stuff like celery, mushrooms, radishes, and cabbage. Also, pay particular heed to crabapples, periwinkle, navelwort, elderberry, and sweet cicely; especially the last one.

What can you do about it? Well, you can learn to cook. Don't snicker. You had better unless, of course, you want to spend your nights in restaurants, and in today's financial climate, that would mean you go from dinner to your second job to pay for that dinner. Don't pooh-pooh the cooking bit. Do you want to live on sandwiches or TV dinners for nine months? You had better take stock of yourself and the refrigerator.

What then is the bottom line? Well, your wife will gain the normal baby weight, plus a little more. Her cheeks will be rosy, her sleep will be sound, her stomach will be gurgling contentedly. And you? You will lose weight or you will gain weight. Make no mistake about it. You will sleep fitfully. Your stomach will either growl incessantly or feel as though there is a bowling ball made of eggplant inside. The only recourse? Walk the dog. You don't have a dog? Get one. Walk him right on down to Clancy's or McDonald's. Load up. The life you save may be your own.

Summary

The initial third of the pregnancy is a time of exploration. You have been handed a fact that in less than a year, your life will undergo certain basic changes. For one, you will have an additional responsibility. Therefore, it is vitally important that you begin this pregnancy on the right road. There will be plenty to do and you will find yourself in newer and stranger situations as the days roll by. Utilize these first few months wisely. Get the answers to your basic questions *now*. Seek out the help you need *now*. Obtain the information you desire *now*.

In other words, lay the groundwork, the foundation on

which you will be building *now*. It is easier to do this at the beginning when there are fewer problems with which to contend. Unless you meet them now, you'll find that later on they will only triple.

It is also a time for enjoyment. Don't let the excitement pass you by. Relax and enjoy each phase. Take each new situation as it arises. Let nature take its course; it will anyway.

Second only to the birth of a child is being told you will be expecting a child. Soak up the good feelings. Share them with your mate. Remember, it's not just her baby, it's yours too. This baby is part of you both.

Chapter 2:
Months 4, 5, & 6

After the initial excitement of the first three months, these middle innings take on the outward characteristics of Restville, a kind of lull before the storm. Actually, they are nothing of the sort. They are really the bridge between the headiness and newness of months 1, 2, and 3 and the flurry of activity which will make up months 7, 8, and 9.

If you have followed the suggestions in the previous section, then you should find these three months more relaxing. It will be the time for you to sit back and think about all those little things preparatory to the final onslaught. These consist of picking names for the baby, rearranging your sex habits as the old ones have proven useless now that her stomach is in the bulge position, doing daily exercises with her, buying clothes for her, and helping to select the method of delivery.

What, you say, that doesn't sound too relaxing?

You're right. These three months are nothing more than a continuation of what happened before except that new elements have been added. For example, when we last left ourselves, we had been deprived of our butterscotch krimpets. We were on our way to Burger King to have it our way. The problem is your lady fair will be joining you and the situation will worsen when she realizes that the tight-fitting Wranglers she used to wear with pride now look as though they would only fit on a ten-year-old. Like it or not, this fact will have a direct bearing on *your* life.

Clothes 'n' Things

During this next three-month period, the woman will undergo what is loosely termed a "traumatic experience" concerning her appearance. She will find that when it comes to her image, everything that once looked so good will now look not so good.

At the beginning of the pregnancy, it was probably a treat for her to wear blousy, full clothes, saying to the world, "Hey, look, I'm expecting." But, after awhile, these outbursts of pretension change. They change because the initial enthusiasm wanes. It is no longer novel, no longer original, no longer that much fun to troop around the supermarket in tent dresses, especially when about twenty extra pounds are also being carted along. In its place come moments of remorse as she looks down at the sputnik bulging out of her front or feels around to touch her own portable caboose.

It is not an amusing sight and it certainly is not all that flattering—at least to her. So, what happens? The first order of the day is to put those outrageous size fives away in the closet to wait for the body's return to what it deems normal. In this respect, you can be of some assistance. Help her pack those clothes away. Don't just let them hang in the front of the closet for her to see every time she opens the door. Help get them into opaque garment bags and get those bags out of sight. Of course, don't let her forget they

58

are there. It can get mighty expensive furnishing her wardrobe after the birth of the baby.

Somewhere around the fourth month, the necessity for maternity clothes begins. Some women may not 'show' (meaning the start of the swollen abdomen) until later months, but the average is the fourth. Here is where you must step in with a firm foot and a cool head.

Whether or not you have a clotheshorse as a mate, tact is of the utmost importance. You can hardly go around the house saying, "Hey Maura, you sure are getting fat," or "Annie, that dress doesn't fit you like it used to," or "Oh my gosh, Patsy, you've split your seams—all of them."

These will be trying times, that's for sure. But like everything else you have read in this book, you must be able to keep your head about you. If you don't, you may find it stuffed into one of your empty pockets. This especially applies to clothes. She will immediately feel she has to go out and buy herself a whole new wardrobe. And I mean a whole new wardrobe. This is not only unsettling from the emotional standpoint (to her), but it's sure as hell costly (to you).

There is no way to avoid the situation. You can't expect her not to have clothes and you can't expect her not to have clothes which fit. Do you really believe she will put on that little something you picked up from the army and navy store? You know, that green canvas job?

She needs something pretty, something flattering, something that will make her forget, even for one brief moment, that she is slowly but surely becoming a two-legged cow.

All right then, what happens? You can't give her a blank check and hope she will leave something in the account so that you can buy tomorrow's help-wanted ads. That is too dangerous a method because she will leave you just that amount. No matter what you may have heard and no matter what you may have read, maternity clothes are expensive. In fact, they are more than just expensive, they are outrageous. Maternity clothes are stratospheric in cost. This has nothing to do with the fact that more material is used. With maternity apparel, the makers know they have a captured audience. Where else can she go? What else can she do when pregnant? She needs clothes and the only clothes which will fit the shape of pregnancy are what is termed "maternity clothes."

Where do you get these items of necessity? There are certain alternatives here. Let's take them in some order of unimportance:

She can be taught to sew. You can buy her a sewing machine and hope for the best. If she's carrying during the summer months, meaning that the fattest part will take itself over the hot weather, then all she really needs are tentlike dresses. It becomes simply a matter of buying the necessary material and sewing a couple of big flaps together. With a sewing machine, you will also have an investment in the future as a hedge against the increasing encroachment of the local tailor. She can take in your pants, take out your pants, mend the rips, and sew new buttons on that twenty-year-old sports jacket of yours.

You can get involved in what is called the acquisition of "yenims" (pronounced "Yen-Em"). What is a yenim? Let me give you an example.

I am the oldest of three sons. My father has given me a suit which he says he no longer enjoys wearing. Brown turns him off. The suit fits me perfectly. I like brown. After a few years, my younger brother gets down to my size and I turn the suit over to him. He wears it and after a while forwards it to my youngest brother. This is a pass-me-down affair (different from Passover) and, consequently, the garment is given a great deal of use. In fact, this is one of the best illustrations of the use of a yenim. A yenim, then, is a hand-me-down.

One caveat: Friends and relatives may offer to *loan* her clothes. More than likely, she won't wear them and they'll sit in her closet for nine months collecting dust. If she decides to take anything, be sure it fits her and that she looks good in it. Remember, you may get what you pay for.

Dismiss the entire situation and try to cope with the matter *au naturel*. In other words, she stays locked up in the house. This method follows in that great Italian tradition of keeping the wife home, in the kitchen, barefoot, and pregnant. It just takes it a step further.

Clothes are bought. The last resort.

There are shops specializing in only maternity clothes. They have everything from bathing suits to evening gowns, all catered to the pregnant form. You can also shop in some of the larger department stores but, frankly, their selection is not all that great; at least not for what you will be paying. As of now, maternity clothes will run you a pretty penny. For instance, if your wife is used to paying $16 for a blouse at Gimbels, she will be paying $25 for one at a maternity shop. For a dress usually costing $40, figure the maternity special will be around $60. Bathing suits? $45. And the beat goes on.

There is, though, something of an alternative to paying these prices. There are some discount maternity shops around which carry seconds, irregulars, and slightly used garments, so look for them *first*. They may save you a lot of money.

One thing you should understand about all this is the tendency to sidestep what are called nonessentials and nonmixables. Nonessentials don't need a definition: It's simply something she doesn't need, like a $60 bathing suit when you have a checking account balance of $30 and you live in Nome, Alaska. However, what is a nonmixable? It's buying a dark green blouse with yellow trim and light pink slacks with purple stitching. They just don't seem to square up to each other.

When buying maternity clothes, she should try and look for something that she can wear now and which she can rearrange and still wear now and rearrange again and wear later. This means buying slacks and blouses which are interchangeable. For example, a pair of light brown slacks and a pair of dark blue slacks, which can be worn with a light green blouse or an off-white blouse.

Point of information. Maternity slacks are quite different from regular ones. They have a waistband in the front and a square of what appears to be elastic material. This frontispiece spreads out considerably. The purpose? To hold the baby as it grows. An ingenious idea.

One thing I forgot to mention. If you've got a working wife, she will have a tendency to steer clear of all the points above except the last one. She will demand to buy herself anything she needs. The rationale is that she is earning an income. That's a tough argument. However, you can make suggestions as I've indicated. That's why it's good to know about these things.

The tent dresses I mentioned before are pretty good buys, especially at times when these dresses are in vogue; then it seems as if the entire female population is pregnant. What a lifesaver. A couple of those with multicolored scarves and she's in business. Also, make sure she has comfortable low-heeled shoes and support stockings. The reasons are obvious.

The entire concept of maternity clothes has always come

under the heading of Supply and Demand. You supply her with what she demands. But it needn't be that way. Try and follow some of the guidelines I have set forth. It'll save you money and aggravation.

When you do decide to buy maternity clothes, buy them early enough. Don't wait until she goes into the ninth month and then run helter-skelter spreading green all over town. Shop wisely. This way, she'll have full use of the garments over the entire pregnancy period.

Additionally, you will no doubt find that your spouse will begin to accumulate all kinds of lotions, ointments, oils, creams, cleansers, conditioners, moisturizers, perfumes, colognes, and lipsticks imaginable to offset her feelings of fatness. To a woman, a long, leisurely peppermint-tea bath, followed by a liberal sprinkling of a rose-scented powder and punctuated by dabs of Chanel No 5 at strategic points, is heaven. It makes her feel sensual, pretty, and fresh.

So, do yourself and her a favor. Go to your favorite drugstore. Buy one of those kits which include certain basics like lotion, powder, conditioner, and cologne in a handsome carrying bag. Present it to her. Not only will it make her smile, but it will save you big bucks later on. If you don't, be prepared for an avalanche of just about every jar, tube, and bottle produced with just about every cosmetic made.

If you're a male chauvinist, remember the words of Margaret Fishback in her book, *Time for a Quick One*:

Women are wacky. Women are vain.
They'd rather be pretty than have a good brain.

Now, while all this is going on, what happens to you? What happens to *your* clothes?

Other than their disappearing from general lack of care

and your losing some of your favorite shirts to her (she'll be wearing them as overblouses), you will find that clothes will not be of the utmost importance to you. You will not be concerned about having a new suit. You will continue to wear that old ratty tie. You will look the other way when people say, "ring around the frazzled collar." Clothes will have little significance for you. Why? One simple, yet concrete reason. You won't have any money left.

The Cash Flow

One of the things which nag at most men, in fact, practically all the ones I have spoken to, is money. Fritzi Kallop, of the Preparation for Parenthood Program at New York's Lying-In Hospital, says that in her experience there is a genuine concern over money. "The men we had in our classes were, for the most part, worried about their financial responsibilities. How do I support everyone is the hue and cry."

You should at this point consider what this whole episode will cost you. I don't mean just the clothes. You have already noted that one hefty expense will be the obstetrician and the hospital. Add to that clothes and medication for the mother and clothes, medication, and furniture for the baby, and you will see an even healthier sum.

All right, let's not panic.

Once more we retreat to the basement. Bring with you the bank books and the insurance policies. Sit down before a desk or table. Clear it of everything except maybe a calculator, a big piece of paper, and lots of pencils and erasers. Make two columns on that big piece of paper. On one side, under the heading of "Assets," list all the money you have in your checking and savings accounts, or anywhere else for that matter. Figure out what your present net income is. This may not be limited solely to you.

One of the first things to be considered is whether the mother-to-be is planning to work or continue to work. If she is now working, but will be stopping, what kind of maternity leave does her company provide? Any severance pay? If she intends returning to work after the baby is born, what are the feelings you both have on child care? What does it cost in your area?

If she doesn't return to work, then you will have to compute what effect the lack of the second paycheck will have on your household, especially with the new addition. Can you swing it? If not, then alternative methods may have to be taken, whether they involve your looking for a new, higher-paying job or a second job, or moving to cheaper accommodations.

Now, from the income only, subtract your fixed monthly expenses; i.e., rent, telephone, electric, food, etc. Forget about your Tuesday night poker game or the Saturday night theater or the two-week vacation in Portugal. They may all have to be modified somewhat.

The balance, coupled with what is presently in the bank accounts (and from any other sources) is what you have to bring this baby home. While you're at it, review your medical insurance policies. Find out how much the insurance carrier will pick up and what procedures are involved. If specific forms are needed or certain information is to be supplied, then obtain it now. Don't wait until the last moment and then go scurrying around. The sooner the forms are completed and the necessary information is furnished to the insurance people, the sooner you will receive your reimbursement.

Okay, what's this baby going to cost you?

These figures go on the "Debit" side of the ledger. Remember, the numbers may vary, depending on where you live. Also, some of the specific items I mention may be gifts from family and friends. What I am listing here is what it will cost you if you get no relief.

Medical

Obstetrician	$ 700
Circumcision for a boy	50
Hospital: 4 days, semi-private room	1,000
Pediatrician's visits to hospital	50

Maternity Clothes

3 tent dresses	100
2 slacks and 4 blouses	125
3 bras	25
2 prs. shoes	30
stockings, misc. apparel	50

Medication	30

Baby's Things

Layette (See Chapter 3 for specifics)	150
Toiletries (including diapers)	75
*Furniture:	
Crib with mattress and bumpers	225
Dressing table	75
Carriage	85
Room humidifier	25
Infant seat	20
Nurse, (if needed—2 weeks)	250

Total: $3,065

---

* Initial needs. Playpens, high chairs, strollers, etc., come later.

Don't let it get to you. Remember, the sums paid to the doctor and the hospital are medical expenses on your tax return, to the extent you have not been reimbursed by insurance. And the baby? That's a new $750 tax deduction, or $1,500 if you have twins.

More Physical Changes

By the time you pick your head up from the desk, you will undoubtedly notice that your wife is much bigger than she was when you first went down the stairs. You will quickly see that as her anterior enlarges, her posterior expands. The rear section will dip out and "hang" (according to the eminent baby books) because your baby is sitting on her bladder.

Actually, the lady has gained close to fifteen pounds and the uterus which houses your child has now reached the navel. You cannot make fun of this situation. You could get a poke in the nose for such wit.

What can you do? Nothing. If you have empathy, some kind of sympathy, you can stoop your shoulders, slump forward in a rounded, obsequious position, and stick out your keester. She will either laugh or clench her fists.

The physical changes in her will not taper off.

"I began to wonder if she would ever return to normal. She always seemed to be getting bigger and bigger."

"She was almost as big as I am. Great. I had somebody to eat with."

She will continue to get fatter. She will continue to sleep more. She will continue to find it more and more difficult to do things for herself. And you? You will continue to spend less time in bed (sleeping, or otherwise) and you will continue to find you are doing more and more.

These are the basic physical changes in both of you.

Understand that all these changes are temporary. In a few months, she will no longer be that fat. In a few months, she will no longer be that tired, and in a few months, she should be able to do more and more for herself and for you (you hope).

So, where does that leave you? Precisely where it left you at the beginning of this section. Nowhere. Therefore, what can you do about all this? Frankly? Without horsing around? Without trying to find an excuse or alibi or reach for some fantastic solution? Very little. You can always cut out, but that will probably bring you a bullet of guilt in the back. You can get help, which will cost. Or, you can try and do as much for yourself as you can.

I found that the best bet was to fudge it, to try and circle the practical problems with a combination of realistic strategies.

Do cut out when she asks you to bring her a third glass of milk in fifteen minutes. Tell her she must get the exercise. A walk to the refrigerator is good for her. Actually, you're not lying; it is.

Get her mother or some friend over to cook dinner at least once a week. Her mother? You can grin and bear it for an hour. Remember those TV dinners?

Try to do some things yourself. It's not really hard to throw a load of wash in the machine. Look at the television commercials for instructions. You also don't have to be a mental giant to figure out how to take your shirts to the laundry and you should easily be able to switch on the vacuum, even if it's only once every other week.

The fundamental thing to keep in mind is to work together with the mother-to-be, even if the share at this time seems disproportionate. After all, consider what's going on inside her.

A Special Report from the Inside—Fifth Month

The growth of the fetus is moving along quite rapidly now. It weighs about fifteen ounces and is approximately seven inches long. Fingernails and toenails are developing. It waves its arms, wriggles its toes, smacks its lips, and moves its eyes from side to side. The spine and chest are now apparent. In fact, the doctor can hear the heartbeat, a heart which pumps fifty pints of blood a day. He can also feel which part of the body is the head, which is the rear, which are the limbs.

The fetus does make sounds. For one, it can hiccough. It even has waking moments and sleeping moments and can easily be startled by loud noises or by sudden movements of the mother.

Incidentally, if you've got more than one kid in there, the doctor can probably detect this by the stethoscopic examination.

Sex and You: Part 2

As long as we are talking about the growth of her physically, both inside and out, we should consider where sex comes into the picture. This period can be the most awkward but it is also the choicest time of all.

At this juncture, her abdomen is starting to bulge. Also, her breasts begin to balloon. As I said previously, the fetus is expected to hold. All systems are go. Your mate is under constant surveillance by her doctor. She is consuming those big, pink pills and she is eating a healthy diet. In other words, she should be in the best condition of her life.

Okay, so what's your problem? You have her where you

want her. Look, she's happy. See those loving eyes? Whatever anger she may have had for your putting her in this shape is gone. She is looking and feeling better than ever before. The paleness which was once in her cheeks has given way to a rosiness. The bloppiness which she experienced before is no longer serving as an excuse for the absence of sex. She will now be technically entitled to wear those tents they call maternity dresses and have a quasi-legal right to any seat on the bus. All she has to do is point her stomach at the man sitting in that seat.

With these things going for her, including the adoration of friends and family, she should become an easy mark for your affections. Look at it this way. Aren't you the one responsible for all those good feelings and all these good looks?

Again, what's your problem? I see your eyes are looking down at the floor. A fear of hurting what is inside her? This concern, according to the medical people, is a normal one. The doctors say that men frequently develop a fantasy they will be harming the baby. However, the fear is an unfounded one. The fact is that sex at this time is harmless to the fetus. If you want to explore this in greater detail, you would find that there are even some religions which claim that women should be left totally by themselves during pregnancy; their bodies and their minds should not be disturbed. Okay, we don't have to go that far but intercourse during pregnancy still has to be treated with some sort of sanity. For example, if there is no disease apparent or the woman has not gone through previous miscarriages, then intercourse can proceed normally.

What is normal, of course, may differ depending on the woman's physical and mental condition. But the bottom line is that during this period of the pregnancy no harm can come to the baby from intercourse. And when I say that, I include the introduction of semen into her. It will not reach the baby. It can't. Remember, that child of yours is surrounded by a first class, Grade A sac which cushions it and protects it magnificently.

All right, now that we have gotten that out of the way, there are a few things to consider from the woman's physical and emotional points of view.

One aspect is your approach. Go back to those courting days. Bring her flowers. Tell her how fantastic she looks. Subconsciously she already believes this anyway and what you are doing is reinforcing such beliefs, thus, easing the path. Besides, the three-month period which will follow may be so horrendous that you had better do everything you possibly can to ensure peaceful coexistence when you enter the homestretch.

During this middle period, she should be most receptive to just about everything except the gymnastics of the pre-preg days. The bulge in her abdomen will not be that pronounced or so uncomfortable to her that you can't still use the missionary position. It also will not be protruding so that you can't side-by-side it. If she's like most women, she will probably prefer the reverse missionary position where she becomes Dr. Livingstone and you become the native, primarily because it is comfortable and let's not ruin anything she finds comfortable, eh Gaspard?

What you really have at this stage is an exchange of those positions which require a gymnast with those which require an aging lothario. Smoothness, care, tenderness, and a great deal of charm are the orders of the night.

It won't really be as difficult as it sounds. Your wife will generally be agreeable to all your advances. In fact, she will often be the one taking the offensive. Don't forget that. She

71

still wants to feel she is needed and desired, and as long as she is snuggling up to you, then all you really have to do is respond, leaving the rest to Father Nature. All right, I admit it won't be rough and tumble stuff, but let's not be too greedy. How would you like to be shut out for the entire nine innings?

One positive aspect should come out of this: Providing the couple is willing, there should be an expansion of the sex act. That's right. Pregnancy affords a couple a golden opportunity to experiment. They can try new positions and techniques which will add spice to their love lives later on. Because of her condition, these new positions may be advisable and some of them may prove surprisingly interesting.

Positions

Somebody once told me that during pregnancy, there were a whole host of new and inventive positions. I thought she was kidding but she proved otherwise.

It is often said that the best position and the easiest for the woman is side-to-side. I find it rather intriguing how one is supposed to bypass a protruding eight inches of stomach. I mean, we could try stretching ourselves but what we have isn't exactly a rubber band. This side thing has to be for the birds, who may be the only ones able to do it that way.

Now, what kind of positions can you utilize:

1. The woman can lie on her back with her leg across your thighs. This astride position is particularly effective since the woman can control the depth of penetration and can remove any psychological fears of damage to her.
2. She can sit on the edge of the bed and then bring her legs up to your shoulders. In effect, she is using your shoul-

ders as a kind of foot rest, which affords her support and which affords you a way around the bulge in her middle.

3. The "X" position is where she sits on your lap facing you, legs astride. You simply keep your legs straight. It works best on a bed, not a chair.

4. Reverse "X," where she sits on your lap with her back to you. A chair is okay here.

5. Rear entry. Exactly what it says. It can also go both ways; that is, entry into the vagina from the rear as well as entry into the rear from the rear. Don't knock it until you've tried it.

Additionally, keep in mind that there is certainly room for manual and oral sex, not to mention masturbation. Experimentation is extremely important and given some basic positions and an eagerness to succeed, you can improvise to your heart's content.

"How much sex can I expect?" you ask. It must be understood that there is no hard and fast answer to this question. As the cliché goes, "Different strokes for different folks." What you have to remember is that it is not necessarily a bad thing or an abnormal way of behaving if you have less sex than you might think you should have. In fact, research even shows that there is nothing inherently wrong or abnormal if there is no sex at all during pregnancy. In other words, don't feel guilty about whatever you are or are not doing. If you do encounter guilt, understand that it may be solely of your own doing and then find out why you have such feelings.

By now, you must realize that some of these new ways to have sex require you to be either somewhat double-jointed or in reasonably good physical shape. Most of us would have to strive for the latter condition. So . . .

The Expectant Father's Survival Kit

Exercising

Peter Gennaro, the well-known choreographer and dancer, once said this in an interview with me:

> Exercise is not a monthly routine. It's not something you do just to get rid of certain excess weight and once that is accomplished, well, goodbye, so long and fare-thee-well.
>
> No, it's a lifetime activity and once you begin to make it a part of your daily living, you'll find it'll go a long way. You're also apt to break and strain less, both bone and muscle. Your body will be supple, flexible, like a baby's and when you fall, well, there would be more elasticity to spring back rather than the awesome sound of plop, snap and crack.
>
> Look at it this way. A body was not made to get up, have fourteen bagels with cream cheese and sit in a chair all day and watch *Hollywood Squares.* It was made to read and watch and laugh and sing and hop and play and run and . . .

Exercises. Also known as workouts, calisthenics, gymnastics. It is important that your spouse gets into some sort of exercise routine. Why? First, it is helpful to her condition. It will prevent her from getting too flabby and too soft. More importantly, it will keep the blood circulating well and all systems running A-okay. This is needed during the lethargic and cumbersome times of pregnancy.

Secondly, exercising will decrease the chances of what happens to her body after the baby comes. We all know the ads which proclaim, "Know how you can lose twenty pounds?" and then in smaller type beneath, "Have a baby." That's fine and dandy for the product that is being sold; however, it doesn't mean much for your gal.

When she gets through popping out that baby, she will still be left with a great deal of flab. So, if you're looking for a body pretty much like the one you remember at the time of conception, or even better, it behooves you to check into this exercise thing with her.

Of course, there are some women who do not take to being told to exercise, or believe that they even need it. Also, women do not especially like to stretch and bend alone. Anyway you look at it, it is always easier to exercise when there are people around. Go into any gym and see how many guys work out solo. Most of the time, people stretch with other people. This way, they can kvetch together.

"Oh, I'm dying. Look at me, Ralph, am I not dying? One more pushup. Ah, done. See that, Ralph? Three pushups today." Or,

"Hey, Artie, watch this situp. Oomph. Wait, don't go away, Artie. I'm getting it. I almost have it. Don't go away."

Far better to work your misery in the company of others. You know what this means? Right. It means you've got to include yourself.

Okay, I have heard all the complaints. I have heard all the alibis. I have heard it all. Exercising ain't no fun. I don't think it was intended to be fun anyway. The plethora of exercise books which have glutted the marketplace make you do everything and anything at the same time, while smiling no less. They twist you around like a pretzel and then walk away.

What am I recommending? Forget all those crazy calisthenic books. Use a basic concept of limbering, stretching, and loosening. Walk, bicycle, swim, jog; in fact, anything that turns you on, even sex. Stretch and work and utilize what you have. There is no right and wrong way. It's just a matter of getting something done.

Remember, you're not trying out for the Olympics. The intention is to stretch your body, to put those unused muscles to work. The objective is for you to use your body naturally, not to torture your bones. Don't forget that muscle and fat are attached to those bones. The secret is not in the number of exercises you do, but in the regularity with which you do them.

What makes me such a maven on the subject? I'm an ex-Parris Island/Camp Lejeune leatherneck who instructed recruits in the fine art of grunting and growling. Don't run off. Even the Marine exercises are grounded in very simple, easy-to-do, easy-to-live-with techniques.

Decide, for example, to do ten minutes' worth of exercises at least four times a week. That's not much. If you don't see a vast improvement in your body after three weeks, then ask (or try and ask) the publisher for your money back on this book. Actually, don't expect extraordinary bulging of all your pectoral muscles or even your triceps or biceps. You are not trying to build yourself into Arnold Whatshisname. It won't really work, not without literally thousands of manpower hours, and loads of grease.

That's not the intention anyway. What you should be experiencing is a more comfortable feeling about yourself, a kind of well-being. You know, like the adage, "Healthy Body, Healthy Mind." The key to any kind of exercising is, then, consistency and to some extent, variation.

Varying what you do will give you staying power; that is, will help you retain your interest in what you are doing. Consequently, your exercises should become a part of your living pattern, like brushing your teeth.

Make the exercises simple enough so that the mother-to-be can join with you. That's one of your primary goals. Get her to work with you. Set aside ten minutes just before *Let's*

Make A Deal, or perhaps during the 7 o'clock news. You'd be surprised what you can do while watching Walter Cronkite. Fix a routine and force yourself to stay in it.

You must have realized by the time you got to this page that pregnancy was not a rose garden. Accordingly, you will need to be in top physical and mental condition to get through these trying times and the ones still to come. She is (hopefully) keeping herself in the best condition possible too, but you can help both of you. One way is by exercising.

Now, what about those specific exercises? Simple and easy. Stay with them faithfully and they'll carry you a long way. Also, as I said before, vary them. They don't all have to be done at every session. One final comment. Don't forget to check with your own doctor before you start any kind of exercise program. It is strictly a precautionary measure.

The Magnificent Seven

1. Knee bends
Exactly what it says.

> Hands on hips.
> Heels together.
> Squat down.
> Come back up.

No hurry. Each bend should take about five or six seconds. Get into a rhythm. Do ten of these.

2. Touch toes

> Drop hands in front of you.
> Reach down.
> Touch whatever you can.
> Come back up.

Try and see how far you can get. Stretch, but easy. No pulling, no jerking. Smoothness counts. If you can't touch, don't worry about it. Do five of these.

3. Hip rotation

Hands on hips.
Grind those hips.
Make a circle (as if you were in a discotheque).
Five rotations one way, five the other way.

4. Wrist and arm movements

Arms straight out in the air by your sides.
Shoulder level (like you were an airplane).
Rotate your wrists.
Ten seconds in one direction, ten in the other. Now, the whole arm. Ten one way, ten the other.

5. Situps

Yep, we all know them.
Arms by your sides (don't worry about the arms-behind-the-head routine).
Sit up. (Use your arms to push you up, if necessary).
Do ten of these.

6. Leg bends

Still on your back.
Bring your knees up to your chest.
Straighten them out.
Bend them.
Straighten them out again.
Do ten of these too.

7. Clock time

Stay on your back. Use your arms and legs as the hands on a clock. Try as many hour and minute hand-times as you can with whatever appendage is convenient. A few minutes of these are fine.

See: Easy, clean, quick.

For those of you interested in harder movements, you always have the old favorites: pushups, squat-jumps, leg curls, belly-whoppers. Or, make up your own but never lose sight of what you are trying to do, which is to stretch, loosen, and limber up your body. If you would like to exercise along with pictures, I recommend an interesting book, *Body Works*, by Frank Wagner. It was published in 1974 by Harmony Books. It has a gatefold cover which can be folded back so that the book becomes a stand-up palette.

Don't just read this section and forget it. Remember, a minute of practice is still worth more than an hour of preaching. So get to it.

Naming the Baby

Here's the fun part . . . for other people. For you, it becomes a period of confusion and acute indigestion. Selecting a name for the baby can easily give you a headache, mainly because nobody is really sure what they want in the way of a name or under what circumstances.

It should be noted that you fathers-to-be especially have a predilection for a particular sex and it is usually a son. Why? There have been many reasons put forth by the research people, ranging from wanting to have a playmate to giving you an opportunity to relive your own childhood. Some men just want someone to carry on the family name. But, more about that later. We're talking about names now.

79

Fortunately, the family name does not offer much of a problem. It's the first part that does.

By and large, there is a great deal of pressure applied here, pressure which emanates from a variety of sources. There is religious preference, family preference, friends' preference, your individual preference, and your mate's preference.

You can handle most matters concerning the baby with a minimum of interference, but naming the child is in a category all its own. You will find that during pregnancy, whenever someone meets you, two questions are immediately asked: When is the baby due? And, what's the baby's name going to be?

Some parents-to-be never settle on a name until practically the eleventh hour. There are some, of course, who have always known what the names would be from the very moment of conception. There are some, too, who have no choice, meaning they will be forced to name the baby such-and-such or so-and-so.

Let's separate some of these areas, although there is still considerable overlapping from one into another.

In Western civilization, religion seems to play the dominant role. For example, if you are of the Jewish persuasion (and remember, everything I say here depends on the origin of the prospective mother, too), the baby is usually named after a deceased relative, never one still alive. The request for such a name will come from a living relative, most likely somebody's parent.

"Now, Stuart, you were always your grandfather's favorite. He adored you. He wanted to leave you his car before it got repossessed. The least you can do is name the baby after him."

(As you may have gathered, I speak from firsthand knowledge.)

There is one loophole. My wife and I had previously decided that we would use her maiden name as the baby's middle one, in honor of her mother who had died a few months earlier. My wife's not Jewish. For a first name, we were debating between David or Billy (if a boy) and Kelly (if a girl). We wanted a boy.

My mother likes Kelly but she is concerned over the boy's name. You see, her father (my grandfather) had died a number of years ago and still had not received a name. I must admit I was not too crazy over the name William and the nickname Billy. David was still my favorite. My wife liked both names.

So, if anyone was torn between tradition, a mother, a favorite grandfather, and a name, it was me. And this conflict existed until the time of birth, and then it was quickly resolved as you will see.

In Jewish tradition, when you name a baby after a person, you actually take the name of that person. This does not mean you have to confiscate the exact name. There is a rather complicated set of procedures by which you use the deceased party's English name, translate that into the Hebrew equivalent, transpose that into the proposed moniker and divide by 73.

However, it still comes down to this. If your grandfather's first name was Irving, family pressure will send you looking for a name starting with an "I." This is not as easy as it appears. Remember, you are being limited to one letter of an alphabet of 26. Just take a look at some of the names which begin with "I" for both boys and girls:

There are Ignatius, Igor, and Imre for the males and Ingebord, Iola, and Isolde for the females. And how would you like that beautiful little boy with the pink cheeks and button nose and the dimpled smile to be called "Irving?" (No offense intended.) Of course, if there are two deceased, unnamed relatives, you can split the names; that is, one deceased party getting the baby's first name and one deceased party getting the baby's second or middle name.

In the Christian world, things are a bit simpler. Many times, the child will be named after a living person. For example, a boy might be named after his father; conversely, a girl after her mother. This is sort of a homey arrangement, although there are a number of psychiatrists and psychologists who say that this causes identity problems in adult life. For instance, a child might be named Thomas J. White III. It is obvious what this means. He's the third generation of Thomases in the White family.

The confusion comes into focus when everybody is still alive and kicking. Then, it is not unusual to have Big Tommy, Little Tommy, and somebody (your kid) called Tom-Tom running in and out of the same house. By the same token, an equal number of people feel this arrangement affords closer family identity.

The decision is yours.

When religion is not an issue, there is family preference to be considered. Most of the time it will be exerted from her side by the suggested use of the family name. We all know by now that parenthood is a joint effort and, therefore, the new parents of today will join forces in a name. This means that while the last name may be his, the middle name may be hers. Surnames (or family names) will then be carried forth.

You can also take it a step further by hyphenating the last name: using her maiden name followed by a hyphen and then your last name. Or there is one couple I know who used her maiden name as the child's first name. Again, the preference is a personal one.

There is also individual preference, yours and hers. Rare is the couple who can agree completely on any given name. Taking the different backgrounds and tastes of the parties into consideration, it is not surprising that they turn to the name books in order to find a name which both of them like, let alone trying to satisfy other people.

You might want to mull over a few points when you begin to select the baby's name.

The best thing you can do, and it is certainly not all that easy, is to resist the temptation to follow what everybody else would like. You should be guided by your own instincts and feelings coupled with those of the mother-to-be. This is not a simple task. The easy way out obviously is to let everybody else run the show. At least that is what you may think, but when you see the diversity of opinion even among those people, you will really begin to wonder what road is the least complicated one.

"That's a terrible name," proclaims venerable Aunt Mary, who then goes on to recommend something out of *Star Wars*.

Most people, if you ask them, think that children should have a "proper" name. The only trouble is in the definition of what is proper. For instance, if your name is Ichabod, you may question seriously your mother's suggestion. After all, if she can name her own son Ichabod, what would she do to your kid?

By the same token, it is rather difficult to listen to a well-intentioned father-in-law who helped name his own daughter Hepzibah Triona as the first and second names, which hardly complements the family name of McGarrity.

And then there are those who maintain that any name

which is not a "regular" name (meaning Tom, Bill, Joe, Jim, or Bob) is nothing more than a "perverted attempt at bastardization," whatever that means.

Nobody really knows how many names there are in the world, but there is certainly a wealth of baby books with names in them. You can spend from now until the cows come home sorting out all the ones which are available.

Most people like to pick names which have some sort of meaning. This has a rather nice touch to it. Some people are interested in derivations and meanings. Call a boy William and you have a name of Teutonic origin denoting "resolute defense or resolute helmet." Name him George and you have a Greek origin, meaning "man of the earth."

For girls, ponder this: Nancy is a variant of Hannah and comes from the Hebrew, meaning "grace, mercy." You can even dig a bit deeper. For example, in its original form, the name Nancy was pronounced Kha-nah, with stress on the second syllable. As one nation after another adopted it, changes took place. It now exists in many forms, seventy or more, ranging from the popular Ann to the relatively unknown Annushka.

Some derivations are downright amusing. Consider Thomas, which is derived from the Aramaic Tama or Twofold Twin. The Thomas of the Scriptures was sometimes called Didymus, a Greek name with the same meaning. His mind is said to have been as twofold as his name, causing him to be something of a skeptic; hence the expression "Doubting Thomas."

Again, whatever turns you on.

Some people will go a step further and come up with an artificial name; that is, one which has specifically been invented. (If I give you even one example, I will quickly lose my best friend.)

There are hundreds of different rules which are put forth in the baby books, as well as by parents and friends alike on how names should be picked.

The *New Webster Library of Universal Knowledge* lists seven specific ones:

1. The name should be worthy.
2. It should have a good meaning.
3. It should be original.
4. It should be easy to pronounce.
5. It should be distinctive.
6. It should fit the family name.
7. It should indicate the sex.

Love that last one.

It would seem to me that unless religion has considerable influence on what you do, or you have some fixation with a particular name, there are two simple hints to keep in mind: one, pick a name that the kid will be able to live with; two, make sure it goes with the rest of the kid's name. What do I mean? With all due respect to those who have such a name, I question the reasoning behind naming a baby Percival Chauncey Algernon IV. That kid is not going to thank you later on, especially if he is a she.

Secondly, I always find it rather amusing for a kid to be named Christopher John Rosenblatt. Really, fellows, really.

Remember that old story about the fellow named Stanley Gaborkstead who went to court to change his name? He felt that the name was laughable, silly, and downright inconsistent with his work as a ballet dancer. After considerable hassle, he had the name changed, from Stanley Gaborkstead to Lance Gaborkstead.

There are many rules which you can follow in selecting a

name, but one of my favorites comes from a friend living in the wilds of Chevy Chase, Maryland. She has three boys: Anthony, Emmanuel, and Timothy. Don't ask me what the last name is; you wouldn't believe it.

She always considers one thing whenever a name is proposed: "What will the kid think of it when she's sixty-five?" Sixty-five? You've got to be kidding. Why, *Mrs. Gaborkstead*, of course.

As Socrates said, "The giving of names is no small matter, nor should it be left to chance or to persons of mean abilities."

Methods of Delivery

We are now along the backstretch and getting ready to start the final lap. Before we position ourselves for the turn into the homestretch, we have one more element to consider. We already have the hospital in which the baby is to be delivered. We have the doctor to deliver the baby. We must now give some thought to the different methods of delivery.

You can go bananas reading the literature put out on delivering babies; therefore, you might try asking around, talking with friends, and people you trust and respect. And that includes your obstetrician, first of all.

There are many ways to deliver a baby, some elective, many not. The usual way is known as spontaneous, natural delivery. This means that the baby comes out through the birth canal (vagina). The delivery may or may not be assisted with *forceps*.

The second way is a *caesarean section*, sometimes just called a "section." An incision is made in the abdominal wall and the wall of the uterus. The baby is then lifted out.

86

Months 4, 5, & 6

This is a major operation and is not considered an elective method of delivery. It becomes necessary where there are certain complications internally which mandate a quick removal of the baby, or where there may be physical problems in delivering the child vaginally. Common among these is a large baby and a small pelvic area.

Other delivery techniques may involve *induced labor*, the increasing use of *midwife-nurses*, and for delivery without drugs (spontaneous: without drugs), or *natural childbirth*.

However, let's not get too far along at this point. First of all, let me break down the various methods involved in the birth of a baby, and at the same time put an end to some of the misnomers.

Spontaneous: With Drugs

The approach which you may have heard from the time you were in long pants was the one utilized by your mother. It was known as the "I don't want to know from nothing" view or "Give me gas, quick!" As you would hear it, the woman was wheeled into the delivery room and knocked out. When she awoke, she was back in her room with the baby safely nestled by her side.

This is not quite accurate. Despite all you may have heard and been led to believe, the woman *must* be partly conscious in order to complete the pushing required to expel the baby.

There are various drugs which can be administered to ease the pain. A particularly common one is known as "twilight sleep," which puts the woman in a kind of euphoric state so that she remembers little, if anything, of what went on. This is probably what your mother had; it has been superseded by newer, more modern techniques.

For your information, you should be aware of the fact

87

The Expectant Father's Survival Kit

that there are certain drugs which can be administered to ease the labor pains. Men are not really sure of what kind of pain that is. Some women say it's like intense menstrual cramps. Again, what does that mean to us? What are menstrual cramps like? As best as I can determine, the pain is akin to sharp cramps in the lower abdomen, similar to the kind preceding a good bout of diarrhea, coupled with back pain and pressure on the bladder. (This should make you weak, chock full of fear, and somewhat tense.)

There are specific drugs which can alleviate some of these symptoms. The drugs used in childbirth are divided into two groups: analgesics and anesthetics.

An analgesic reduces pain. One of the most common is Demerol. It is a drug injected into the system which aids in relaxation and in reducing pain. Other drugs with similar relaxation properties include Valium, Librium, and Vistaril.

The second group consists of the anesthetics. An anesthetic eliminates the pain of birth by rendering the patient insensible to that pain. Some are administered as epidurals, numbing the body only from the waist down.

In any event, what has evolved today in modern medicine is a vast array of obstetrical pain-relievers so that no woman has to experience the extent of discomfort which the previous generations had. Discuss the use of all drugs with your doctor, who will be able to advise you on what method is best, not only for the mother's benefit, but for the baby as well.

Delivery by Forceps

Forceps are tongs, sort of like those instruments you use for dishing out spaghetti. The tongs are inserted into the vagina and around the child's head. The baby is then ex-

88

tracted from the mother by use of these instruments. Forceps delivery is generally used when the baby is too far up in the pelvis and is not dropping naturally, or when the doctor feels that the baby is undergoing too much stress in coming out.

Additionally, forceps are used when the mother is having difficulties and it is considered best to get the baby out as quickly as possible. Sometimes the use of forceps is dictated when there has just not been enough progress in labor.

Caesarean

Supposedly, the term came from Julius Caesar. It is believed that Caesar was born this way. As I mentioned on the preceding page, it is a surgical incision of the walls of the abdomen and uterus for delivery of the baby. Most people shudder when they think of such a procedure. Some women feel they will be disfigured for life; some that they have failed to have their baby naturally; some that they will die under the knife.

Nothing could be further from the truth. Caesarean operations are performed when the doctor feels it is absolutely necessary for the benefit of both the mother and the child. One of the commonest reasons is where the baby is just too large for the mother's pelvis and that there might be irreparable damage to the baby by forcing it down through the birth canal.

Some other reasons may be due to complications arising during labor or when the labor itself is going on much too long for the safety and well-being of both mother and baby.

Although a caesarean section is still an operation, it is a relatively simple one. In fact, a section affords the baby a safer entrance into the world than a complicated vaginal delivery. Actually, some doctors say as good an entrance as even the natural, uncomplicated vaginal delivery.

One word of advice though: Don't listen to any old wives' tales. If a caesarean is necessary, then there is no choice. But, understand again that we are no longer in the dark ages or back in Caesar's time. The mother usually won't be in the hospital any longer than if she had delivered via the birth canal.

Induced Labor

This is a way of bringing on labor before it has begun by itself. The reasons for inducing labor may vary. Some are medical; some are not. For example, from a medical standpoint labor may have to be induced if the mother's or baby's safety is at stake for whatever reason is determined by the doctor. A nonmedical reason? Some women may want the labor induced solely for reasons of convenience. She may want the baby born on a certain date or she may have a wedding to go to and wants the baby out before then. There are many, many reasons. Again, some are sane and some are not.

How is labor induced? The method commonly used is the administering of a particular drug such as Pitocin which stimulates the uterine muscles.

Use of a Midwife-Nurse

A midwife-nurse is a nurse who assists in childbirth. Actually, she delivers the child much like an obstetrician. These midwives are not the old "granny women" of the past, but are nurses who have done special postgraduate studies in obstetrics. They are the next best thing to the doctor.

Many women today who have been "screened" medically

as likely to have a straightforward, uncomplicated delivery are utilizing the services of such a midwife. One of the reasons for this is that a midwife generally remains with the woman during the entire labor period, something which many doctors may neither have the patience nor the time nor the inclination to do. A doctor is on call in case of emergencies, however.

To say that the woman in labor is given confidence and support by such a constant, knowledgeable companion would be an understatement. Midwife-nurses could very well be the wave of the future for those expecting uncomplicated deliveries.

Now, what about your participation in labor and delivery? Yes, I did say *your*. Most men know something about the process of delivery. They know what they have seen in the cartoons of the nervous father-to-be pacing the corridors of the waiting room for what seems like an interminable length of time to hear from the doctor's own mouth what is who. To some men this is the best way. It is also one of the easiest ways. But, to many of us today, there is more of an eagerness not only to share in the experience of birth, but to know exactly what is going on. After all, if there is any doubt as to whether that redhaired seven-year-old belongs to you, what better way to make sure with some degree of accuracy (at least from the delivery standpoint) than to be there when he comes out and to watch the tag go around his wrist.

However, that is certainly not the most important reason. As with anything else, it is generally ignorance which prevents a lot of men today from exploring any new areas. One of the most interesting ways is the natural method of childbirth, also known as the Lamaze Method of Psychoprophylactic Technique.

The Expectant Father's Survival Kit

Spontaneous: Without Drugs

I have purposely held this method for last because frankly I'm prejudiced. Through this procedure the father-to-be can become an integral part of the birth process. In fact, according to many sources, including the Preparation for Parenthood Program at New York's Lying-In Hospital, the natural method is the one which at least 50 percent of the women having babies in this country are turning to.

Nancy and I discussed this method of delivery in great detail. We were both in agreement on trying to bring this child into the world without the use of drugs if at all possible.

For the uninitiated among you, let me assure you that I have not exactly been a walking advertisement for the blood bank. I could keel over at the very mention of the word blood, let alone the sight of it. I originally cringed at the thought of my being present at a natural delivery. My mind conjured up scenes of screaming, blood, and gore. It really sounded like fun.

However, on the other hand, when you look at some of the benefits of this form of childbirth, it seems to make a lot of sense, both from the physical and the psychological aspects. As far as the screaming, the blood, and the gore was concerned, I think you will be surprised to learn what I did.

If you're nervous at the idea of this procedure, try and find some friends who have been through it. Ask them what it's like and tell them what you're afraid of. Get some books, too. There are plenty on the market. But, above all, don't let yourself be persuaded against it by people who don't really know what it is. In any event, for those of you who are interested, I have included in Chapter 3 a brief look at this method from one couple's view—ours.

The Leboyer Method

No discussion on delivery would be complete without mentioning the part that relates totally to the baby.

The era of dangling the newborn upside down and slapping the behind to elicit a howl is slowly fading into the past. Nowadays, many obstetricians feel that there should be a greater concern for the one who is emerging from the quiet and darkness of the womb into a room filled with bright lights and loud voices. They are saying that all this noisy activity is an unnecessary trauma for the baby.

One of the innovators of non-traumatic birth is Dr. Frederick Leboyer who invented a new technique of delivery, as explained in his book *Birth Without Violence*. Dr. Leboyer's method involves the use of soft lighting, low voices, a bath of warm water for the newborn accompanied by constant touching and caressing. The purpose is obvious: to minimize, if not overcome, the trauma of birth.

Additionally, you might want to explore other techniques with similar objectives. For example, you can have your baby born to music, if you so desire. Many women now find that certain musical compositions are particularly soothing to them so that they relax more and, hopefully, experience an easier delivery. It is said that this affects not only the mother but the newborn as well.

Doctors too are helping. There is a greater reluctance today to cut the cord immediately after the baby emerges from the mother's body. More and more obstetricians are simply placing the baby on the mother's stomach and letting the newborn rest for a few minutes; in other words, to experience a sense of peace and calm.

The intention of these techniques is simple. As Dr. Leboyer says, "The newborn baby is a mirror, reflecting our image. It is for us to make its entrance into the world a joy."

A Special Report from the Inside—Sixth Month

The baby weighs about one-and-a-half pounds. In fact, if it were born now, it could possibly live in an incubator.

The baby will start to gain weight, probably about four to five pounds over the next two months. Notice, I no longer call it an embryo or fetus. It is rapidly becoming a baby.

During this period, the sac containing the fluid in which the baby is floating begins to harden. As the baby gets bigger, the greater is the need for this natural shock absorber.

The body is now covered with a greasy substance called *vernix*. Fine hair also begins to grow. This hair is called *lanugo* (Latin for wool) and you'll see some of it at the delivery. The length of the baby? Probably about a foot long. The fingernails and toenails have become quite hard and are easily discernible. The bones are rigid and the facial parts well-developed. The limbs too are strong and the grip reflex especially is now evident.

The baby is positioned high up above the mother's navel and she will find it pushing against her stomach, causing frequent heartburn symptoms. It will also be moving around quite a bit and you'll feel it.

Summary

This is the time to put things in order. Clothes are bought. The money situation is reviewed. Names are picked. A method of delivery is discussed and you may be getting your last bit of sex for the next five months.

If you have followed the suggestions in both the first three months and in these three months, you should be ready for the final phase. If you haven't done anything, then you will be in a position of trying to play catch-up ball, which will be extremely difficult to do. It is like going into the fourth quarter against the Montreal Canadiens down by six goals.

About this time, you may start to feel the movement of your baby. If that is not enough to get you off your duff and into action, then you had better pack it in now. Movement, you say? Okay, before we turn for home, let's see what's going on with your child.

Chapter 3:
Months 7, 8, & 9

They who inspire it most are fortunate,
As I am now; but those who feel it most
Are happier still.

—Shelley

These are the months of movement, movement in a number of ways. A lot happens over the next twelve weeks —the remaining twelve weeks—more than you can ever imagine and the excitement and tension will build to unbelievable heights. It's times like these that truly try men's souls. The emotions churn; the humor fades. Oh sure, we can still be flippant all we want about certain aspects of what is happening to the woman in our life. We can watch her balloon out of shape. We can see what fatigue does to her. We can hear her attempt at sleep, flat on her back, unable to turn over, trying desperately to find a comfortable position.

We can see and hear all these things, among many more, and a number of us will be muttering in our beer, "There but for the grace of . . ."

However, the one area that is often overlooked is not what is happening to her, but rather what is happening to you while all of this is going on.

Anxiety Attacks

At the beginning of this book, we mentioned the emotional upheaval in you when you first learned of your impending fatherhood. By now, this upheaval may have manifested itself in other ways.

You may have already settled the question of money, as well as accepting this new responsibility, but the feelings you now have inside may be quite different from what you recognized before. They certainly should be.

For example, it is plausible that your mate may be turning much of her attention elsewhere. She may seem to be centering her whole world around herself and the baby within: It may appear, therefore, that she has less time for you. Nothing abnormal about this, but you must recognize this fact especially as the time of birth draws near. The ninth month is a terror: not knowing when or how it will happen.

She will be more and more anxious as to what is going to transpire. For that matter, don't tell me you haven't experienced any anxiety attacks either? I have spoken to a number of men about the feelings they have during these trying months. They range from not knowing what to do in any given situation to not caring about what to do.

Are you a typical male if you have these reactions? Men usually undergo the same set of feelings. Some may have them in different ways and under different circumstances, while others experience only a few of them. Generally, we all go through certain periods of discomfort.

Here are a few comments from some males around the country:

"She seems totally concerned about her diet and eating those stupid pills. I think she doesn't even know I exist."

This is a common reaction. The male thinks he is being left out. He thinks she's selfish, that she hasn't any time for him.

"I don't know. I just can't seem to do anything right any more. I mean, anything that pleases her."

This may or may not be true. At this point, the woman tends to be extremely irritable and an evening with Robert Redford would probably not please her either. The man has to be careful he doesn't take everything too personally.

"She snaps at me constantly: why don't I do this; why don't I do that. Hey, I'm tired. I've been working all day. Don't I ever get a break? She's home sitting around all day."

Wait a minute! You've got to watch these feelings closely. Is this jealousy raising its head? He's working and she's doing nothing? Or does he want more attention and if so, what kind? A man who is unusually hostile to his wife's pregnancy may be trying to say he is unusually jealous of the unborn child and afraid that it will replace him.

"I think she likes her doctor too much. Much too much."

There it is, the green-eyed monster raises its head. Clearly, the male is insecure about his position. Add to that the fact that he is also responsible for the delivery of what's inside her and you've got some heavy mental conditions to overcome. Ain't nothing abnormal here, but the male should recognize what his feelings are and that he really doesn't have much to worry about. "If," as my friend in Miami would say, "she's going to run off with anyone, statistics show it's gonna be the bellboy from the Fontaine-bleau."

"I'm sick of Kentucky Fried Chicken three times a week."

Of course nobody says you have to eat Kentucky Fried

Chicken three times a week either. Remember, she is not
exactly having the time of her life shlepping around this
baby and at this stage, cooking may not be her prime concern. If you've got a suggestion for something other than
chicken, then make it. You have to take an active role too,
you know. One fellow told me he simply took her out
to "restaurants:" Monday—Burger King; Tuesday—Kentucky Fried Chicken; Wednesday—McDonald's; Thursday
—Pizza Hut; Friday—Fish 'n Chips; Saturday—Roy Rog-
ers; and Sunday—Jade Tang.

"I can tell you what will happen. I can tell you. Don't tell
me. Once that kid comes around here, she'll have even less
time for me. Less, you hear?"

I guess the first question is why doesn't she have time for
you now? In any event, these protestations sound like insecurity of the highest degree. What is he afraid of? That
the baby will replace him? Stop and think about it. Is that
really possible? Again, maybe the boy from the Fontaine-
bleau, but the baby . . . ?

"I don't know from nothing. I spend most of my time at
the office. That's where it's really at."

Sometimes men throw themselves into their work figur-
ing that the best way to be a good father is to succeed at the
job. However, it doesn't always work out that way. Think
about it.

"I wish we could call the whole thing off. I don't like this
game any more."—IR (Brooklyn)

"I agree."—IR's wife

Aha, back to the starting blocks. Remember those comments at the beginning of this book? Perhaps you should
reread them now. It takes patience and understanding to go
through pregnancy as it does when that baby comes into
your house.

As you can see, anxiety emerges in many ways. You can probably add more of your own, but what it really comes down to is an uneasiness in your mind. To put it another way, Fear:

1. She won't love me anymore.
2. The baby will dominate her life.
3. I'm being rejected.
4. I'm being left out.
5. I'm jealous.
6. I'm envious.
7. I'm . . .

Okay, relax. This is all normal. I repeat, all normal reactions. The men I have spoken to have the same kind of problems and they cover a wide range. One chap said it was *her* pregnancy. "My wife is having a baby. I don't get wrapped up in it. I'm not emotional about all this. It's her, not me. I don't alter my plans. If we have another child, I would do the same thing all over again . . . which is nothing. I believe you should live as you would live any other nine months. There's too much of a big deal made of this pregnancy thing. I think it can only hurt a relationship."

Then there is one fellow who went overboard the other way. He became overly protective of his wife so that she could hardly take a step out of the house before he was quickly at her side. When I asked him why he was so protective, his answer was immediate. "Hey, that's sacred territory. What she has in there is of the highest order. That's what it's all about and it is up to me to protect it and that's what I'm doing."

I agree that these are two extremes. Most of us bounce around the middle, sometimes drifting toward one side and then sliding back to the center again before starting toward the other side. What we should be doing during all this slipping around is to recognize what is happening within us and what we can do about all these strange feelings.

Understand that what she is going through at this time is not too dissimilar from what is happening to you. She is experiencing certain fears of her own. For example, will you still love her after the baby comes? Will the baby take all your attention away from her? Will she still be as attractive and as desirable as before?

Just like you, she is also anxious about what will happen and how. After all, while you may be carrying a great deal of the financial load and plenty of the emotional load, she is still carrying the baby.

Thus, we come back to the word Communication. This is really the bedrock of all understanding. If you feel you are being left out for whatever reason, then put those feelings on the table. She may not realize what she is doing, but don't be afraid to communicate with her. Don't try and protect her; similarly, she shouldn't try and protect you.

Talk to each other. Let each of you understand what the other is going through. This is a time to help one another. You are on the same side and that person inside her is part of you both, a result of your joint effort. Stay on the same side.

Sex and You: Part 3

We now come to the real test. This is where they separate the men from the boys. On the one hand, we have the men: sullen, anxious, nervous, angry, frustrated, and totally horny. On the other side, we have the boys: sullen, anxious, nervous, angry, frustrated, and totally horny.

Why? Look at her. She is enormous. A beachball with

legs. Her legs are blue-veined. Her feet swollen. The puffiness in her face is even more pronounced. And there in the middle of her body is a huge, round ball.

Isn't that attractive, men? Especially if she is in this condition during the summer months when you are sitting on the beach watching the firm flesh parade by. What do you do? Take two steps back and punt.

After witnessing this scene for the better part of an hour, you turn to your immediate left, to the chaise lounge next to yours. There lies this beached whale, greased to the core, soaking up the sun, flat on her back in what is supposed to be a bathing suit (Lady Madonna—$45) with these little, blue goggles on her eyes. The big bulge in her center is hopping up and down.

Slowly, you get up. Slowly, you remove your sunglasses, the loose change in your bathing suit, and your white tennis hat. Slowly you put them down on the chair atop *Looking for Mr. Goodbar.* Then, in a deliberate but unobtrusive manner, you walk toward the water's edge. You pause, and after a last long look at a topless eighteen-year-old, you plunge headfirst into the coldest, biggest wave you see.

"Wait a minute," you say. "Wait one moment. You mean to tell me there's no more sex?"

No, I didn't say that, but sex at this point generally begins to slow down. One reason is that it is physically difficult. Another is that notwithstanding all the new positions, sex comes down to your listening to a few of her protestations every time you get in the mood.

1. "Do you want to crush the baby?"
2. "I don't feel like it."
3. "I have to get my eighteen hours of sleep. The doctor says so."
4. "Gas."

5. "I can't stop the hiccups."
6. "The baby's bouncing around. I think she likes the sun."
7. "More gas."
8. "Do you think I should make the spread blue, pink, or yellow?"
9. "Did you know that Michele is also pregnant?"
10. "Still more gas."
11. "Are you sure you love me?"

Now, don't misunderstand me. Sex can still be accomplished but it will be more of an effort and will require a lot of patience on your part.

One thought must be kept in mind and that is, once the baby has dropped down in the womb (which will probably happen around the eighth month), you must be particularly cautious. Check with your doctor as to specifics.

Another thing must also be considered. The bigger she gets, the more she needs to know you love her and still find her attractive. Don't expect sex to be exactly like it was when she wasn't pregnant or even as it was in the past few months. Appreciate instead its different quality. Toward the waning days, sex will be quite a joke so try and hug her a lot—and there will be a lot to hug.

A Special Report from the Inside—Eighth Month
The baby drops down into the pelvis. The uterus drops about two inches. The baby's head is moving toward the position (engagement) it will be in at the time of birth, and can be felt by the doctor in a vaginal examination.

Months 7, 8, & 9

Moving Around

Too much bed and not enough sleep? In more ways than one. There is a principal reason why it is difficult to get any sustained sleep during these latter months of pregnancy. It is a simple one. *They* won't let you. They? Yes, both of them. What happens is this:

It's 3 A.M. You've finally drifted off to dreamland after spending half the night getting her a drink of milk (or water or juice), listening to her complaints, fighting off the latest sales pitches on bassinets, and reviewing once more the choice of names. Now it's three in the morning and you're dead tired. You know that tomorrow will be hell on wheels down at the office. So, what happens?

"Joe. Joe, are you asleep?"

No answer. Joe is fast asleep. Everybody is fast asleep. Everybody except . . .

"Joe. Joe, are you asleep?"

This time an arm jogs you in the ribs. It taps you on the shoulder. No answer. Joe is really fast asleep. So is everybody else except . . .

Again.

"Joe. Joe, are you sure you're asleep?"

The light clicks on. The bed moves like a ship caught in a storm off the Cape of Good Hope.

"What, Emily? What's the matter?" You bolt upright, your eyes searching for the blue bag with the stuff for the hospital. "What's the matter? What? Wh . . . ?"

"Feel this."

"Feel what?"

"This." She motions to the projection in her center, sort of the cabin in the middle of the ship.

"Why?"

"Because he moved."

"Why? Doesn't he know what time it is?"

"He's moving a lot now. He's kicking me. He's punching me."

"He's also keeping me awake."

"Joe, he's your son, or your daughter. It's alive in there. Want to feel?"

You put your hand on the subject. Nothing.

"I don't feel anything."

"Keep it there. Shhh. You'll feel it."

The clock's hands are now at 3:30. Nothing. You roll over to the right. You reach for the light switch. Click!

Five minutes later. Click!

"Feel now. He's doing a tap dance in there."

Again your hand drifts over. *Niente.*

Don't get me wrong. When it happens the first time, it's quite a thrill, but afterwards, well, how many nights can you start that routine of trying to catch a kick or bump. Besides, what's really going on in there anyway? Actually, the baby *is* moving. It will stretch, it will kick, it will flail its arms out. Some babies will be moving around trying to find their thumbs. True. Some are born with a mark on a thumb showing where they've been sucking it.

A baby may do everything from kicking field goals to a pirouette right there in the uterus. Of course, as the baby grows, there will be less and less room for it to move about and that is when the stronger thrusts are felt.

Sometimes, it seems that you are being the subject of a great put-on by the baby. At least, that is what happened to me. Everytime I went to feel a movement, it stopped.

I found that the best way of overcoming this tease was to challenge the kid outright. I would agree to everything. Thus, when the light clicked on and my hand was grabbed toward the bulge, I utilized the world-famous, proven retort:

"Yes, I feel it. It's kicking. It's doing the Hustle. It's doing the Charleston. Now can I go back to sleep?"

"You're awful. He hasn't moved. You have no patience."

At 4 A.M. on a Monday morning, who needs patience? I need sleep.

This continues from the fifth month on. Actually, up until the fourth month, there will be nothing more than flutters. The real bumping and grinding by your offspring will not start until around the fifth. Initially, they will be minimal, almost as if an air bubble had escaped into the stomach. Gradually, the bubble will give way to a more advanced movement, a subtle mambo.

By the time she enters her seventh month, that Latin beat will be pushed aside by a steady rock 'n roll which generally shifts into second gear during the wee hours of the morning. When the ninth month rolls around, your gal will be doing exactly that: rolling around. Your bed should begin to resemble the Atlantic Ocean at high tide and your kid will be at the peak of performance: beating the hell out of her. Fisticuffs start early.

You do have a choice. You can applaud the "little devil's" movement, which might just get you a cold stare and possibly a rap in the mouth, or you can ignore the whole thing. Ignoring does not really mean what it says it does. It connotes, "Yes, I acknowledge what's going on even if I don't feel it all the time." This is also known as compassion or better yet, "making the most of it."

Sometimes, though, you needn't make the most of it. You might be able to clue in to your feelings.

"I got a kick in the head," said one prospective father. "It was amazing."

"Felt funny," said another. "It was life and I helped to create it. I got a warm feeling. Look, she felt it from the time it was conceived, I guess. I was never a part of it. Now I am."

Whatever approach you take, remember that she is not having a picnic. She is getting bigger, the baby is getting bigger and the ants are getting ready to carry off the lunch. What she needs at this stage is complete attention, understanding, and devotion. If you have none of the above, then you better have a good sense of humor.

Natural Childbirth

Studies have shown that one out of every two women now having babies in the United States is using the natural method of childbirth.

Why? Dr. Guttmacher in his book, *Pregnancy, Birth and Family Planning* says it best:

> Couples . . . report a sense of rapture or near mystical bliss. A birth so conducted creates a feeling of togetherness and mutual accomplishment for wife and husband. The father being able to witness and help with his own child's birth and the mother being able to view the whole procedure through a focused mirror on the opposite wall creates a unique, positive life experience.

There are important other reasons, too. For example,

"Our eleven-year-old from my wife's first marriage has a learning disability," says one father. "The doctors feel that there was something during pregnancy and at the time of delivery that caused this, such as the drugs used. So, that's the main reason we're going natural . . . for the baby's health."

But, what is natural childbirth?

There are many definitions and various concepts involved. The medical term for this method is psychoprophylaxis: the prevention of labor pains by psychic means.

It originally started in Russia in the 1940s, but was not made famous until the French physician Dr. Fernand Lamaze adapted its usage. Today it is commonly referred to as the Lamaze Method. The natural childbirth method is nothing that new. What the Russians and French did was to streamline its use. You only have to consider the babies born well before the 1940s and even today in remote parts of the world where the women simply squat down in the fields and pop the children out to realize that the natural form of delivery is indeed quite natural. What in effect is happening is that we are returning to this kind of delivery, but we are reducing the accompanying pain.

What the Lamaze Method does is to educate the woman as to how the body functions and that childbirth is a normal function of the body.

It stresses three things:

1. Physical exercises to strengthen and prepare certain muscles for labor and delivery
2. Concentration exercises to develop control over those muscles in order to achieve and maintain relaxation
3. Breathing exercises to ensure a proper supply of oxygen and to aid in relaxation, thereby decreasing the awareness of discomfort or pain

Although such a technique doesn't mean there will be a painless labor, it does reduce considerably a lot of the sensations. It's really a question of mind over matter and the results have been incredibly successful. The American Society for Psycho-Prophylaxis in Obstetrics as well as other groups find that some 65 percent of the women utilizing natural childbirth say they experienced *no pain whatsoever.* Don't misunderstand me. I'm not pushing this technique on you. I'm just letting you know what's involved.

Fritzi Kallop again: "Sometimes men don't know why they're in the Lamaze childbirth class, but by the end of it they are all very much involved, not only in the actual procedure, but in the excitement of new life and in sharing."

How does this apply to you? When you deal with the natural childbirth method, it means that you can be more than just a witness to what is going on. The best way to explain this is to tell you something about what's involved in such a procedure.

There are many courses and programs available throughout the country. One, for example, is the Preparation for Parenthood Program at the New York Lying-In Hospital. They do not use the term "natural" but prefer to say "planned" or Lamaze. In any event, it has a general philosophy for its program:

> We believe that fear-reducing knowledge of what to expect in labor and delivery, in addition to breathing and relaxation techniques, are the greatest tools that a couple can have in labor.

At Lying-In, the accumulation of this knowledge means one two-hour lesson per week for six weeks. The course begins during the seventh month, which also suggests that somebody is bound to drop out before it is completed. Sort of like playing Russian roulette with the uterus.

If you decide to take any of these natural childbirth

courses, you should understand that the course itself generally breaks down into certain key components. Naturally, some courses may emphasize some areas more than others or may incorporate different matters, but for the most part you will be confronted with the following:

1. A complete analysis of what happened—that is, how she became pregnant and what is happening inside the uterus.
2. The basic discomforts during pregnancy, plus a discourse on various analgesics and anesthetics in childbirth.
3. A tour of the hospital facilities so that you know exactly where you are going when the due date arrives.
4. Breathing techniques. This is the heart of the naural childbirth method.

I think you will be able to get a better idea of what this course consists of by my taking you briefly through some of the paces. As I said before, the course given in your area may differ, but basically it consists of these elements: information and exercises. The anxiety is supplied by you.

Take my first exposure to the hospital. A large room bedecked with charts, graphs, and whatnots. On one wall there is a bulletin board advertising the latest in baby needs: Bouncinettes imported from Australia for the baby to bounce in; Snuglis from the wilds of Colorado for the baby to be carried in; all-cotton sleepers from France for the baby to sleep in; Pampers from Cincinnati for the baby to . . . On another wall is a complete listing of every service imaginable: baby-sitting, parent-sitting, diaper services, breast-feeding. You name it; they've got it.

The remaining walls are plastered with pictures of babies being born, the proud mama crying her heart out with joy

—not pain—and the proud papa clicking away on his borrowed Nikon.

There are about a dozen couples in the class. For the most part, the women are in their late twenties to early thirties and this is their first baby. They are eager, anxious, excited, and friendly. The men are generally in their late thirties or early forties. They are, they are . . . out of focus.

The first time you attend such a class is akin to the first round in a fight: a feeling-out process. You're eyeing the other people. Are all these women as fat as yours? Are the guys also bearing that frightened, glazed look? Very little, if anything, of the first lecture seems to mean much. The instructress (rarely do you have a male teacher) dabbles in how you got into this predicament and then explains the Lamaze Method in great detail.

It is, however, the second lesson where things begin to pick up, for it is here that the first of the relaxation techniques are offered. Relaxation for the women, yes, but for the guys? Oy vey! Picture, if you will, this slim instructress. She is about twenty-two years of age, 5′5″ tall, weighs a solid one-hundred-and-ten pounds, has long red hair, a cute button nose, full ripe lips, and a figure representing the best of Sophia Loren, Anita Ekberg, and Raquel Welch.

She is sitting on a rug in the center of the room, Indian-fashion. Surrounding her are the pregnant ladies. All are supposed to be in slacks, except that there is always one who shows up in a dress and she is constantly trying to keep her panties from showing.

Why is this important to mention? Remember, you are wallowing in the seventh month. Your gal is out to here. She sleeps on her back, snoring up at the ceiling. She can no longer see her feet. She also feels as though she will always look this way. Those tight-fitting Wranglers are surrounded by cobwebs. She doesn't think she will ever get back into them again. Your sex life should, at this point, be at a standstill. If it's not, then either she's not pregnant or you are doing something uncommonly right.

Back to the scene: twelve guys sitting on chairs surrounding a circle of fat women who in turn surround a piece of lusciousness.

I am sitting there contemplating my hangnail. The next voice you hear is that of the instructress:

"Now, ladies, the first order of business is to get you doing the proper exercises which you will need during labor and delivery. All right, we will slowly contract each of the pelvic muscles: the rectum, the urethra, and the vagina. "Okay, squeeze tight on your rectum. Count to five. Good."

I look at the fellow to my right. He is edging toward the end of his seat, his red tie dropping in front of him like a long, fat tongue.

"Now, ladies, squeeze tight on your vagina. Bring it up in the air. Count one-two-three-four-five, as if you were in an elevator stopping at each floor from one to five. Bring it up. That's it."

I look at the fellow to my left. He has just crossed and criss-crossed his legs fourteen times in the past five seconds. He has a pained expression.

"Now, ladies, hold this at five for several seconds and then slowly relax the pelvic floor muscles as you are coming back down on the elevator. Five-four-three-two-one."

My heart quickens. I begin to feel dizzy. Somebody asks a question. I think it's the one with the suede shoes sitting at the far end of the room. He wants to know how many times a day his wife should do this exercise (the sadist) and what all this raising and lowering of the pelvic area means (the masochist).

The instructress explains:

"She should be doing this fifty to sixty times a day. Contracting and relaxing these muscles prepares the pelvic floor for labor and delivery. This is an important exercise to be done throughout a woman's life to maintain support of the pelvic organs and to help prevent complications from delivery that may not occur for many years."

"Do I have to be with her for these exercises?" he asks. Oh, the imbecile!

"Now that's a good question and something I wanted to remind you about. Actually, I would suggest you work with your wife on this. Although it is not necessary, I think that in the state she is in, both physically and mentally, it would be a nice gesture."

Nice gesture? Would you believe this? Fifty to sixty times a day watching rectums, urethras, and vaginas being lifted and squeezed and lifted and squeezed . . . Ohhhhhh! Which way to the monastery?

I will not bore you with the other kinds of exercises learned at this second session. They are similar in nature and unless your sexual adrenalin will enable you to stay at bay, you had best keep as far away from these practice sessions as is possible. The reason behind the exercises such as the one just mentioned is obvious. It is like the exercise athletes go through. As a pitcher warms up his arm, so too a woman warms up her pelvic area in order to keep it loose and relaxed, thus making the muscles more elastic so that they stretch a bit easier as the baby is being born.

All right, once we pass this exercise position, in which you really have little to do, we come to the area where your talents are needed the most. When I say needed, I really mean it. This has to do with the breathing and relaxation techniques. Interestingly enough, they are quite meaningful because their usefulness is not limited to women. Men can also benefit from these techniques inasmuch as they concern the entire body, not just the pelvic area.

Here is where you come into the play. You are termed the "Coach." What does a coach do? Exactly what you would think. He becomes the advisor, the helper, the guiding light, the inspiration.

You will note that in the natural childbirth method, there is great emphasis on the help of the male. In fact, so great is the emphasis that the man works right along with the woman on the breathing exercises. That's right. What she does, he does—in practice, that is. When it comes to actual labor and delivery, he'll have his hands full with other matters.

The object of all these exercises, which consist of breathing and concentration, is to develop an ability to relax, to listen to commands, and to ride the crest of the contractions.

So that we don't get too far away from the field, there is included a section following this one on obstetrical terms which should answer everything you may want to know or need to know about what is going on. Contractions are simply the movement of the uterus in forcing the baby out.

According to the Lamaze theory, concentration (the mind) will control the matter (the physical). It is not my intention to get into all the exercises involved because most books on childbirth have them and what's the sense of repeating things if they don't have a *direct* effect on you? One book on this subject that I would particularly recommend is *The New Childbirth* by Erna Wright. There's a paperback edition put out by Pocket Books.

The breathing exercises which make up the natural childbirth method are varied and their intention is to control the contractual pain. These same exercises can also be used by anyone (male or female) in daily life.

For example, ever get that cramped feeling in your stomach, either caused by too much work, too little work, work you hate, people you hate, or the usual rigmarole of everyday living? Well, there is a particular breathing exercise which alleviates this tightness. Incredible as it sounds, it does work.

Try this. Focus your eyes on a small, immobile object. Take that empty bottle of Schlitz over there. Now, take a deep breath through your nose and exhale it through your mouth. Do four of these every five seconds or eight every ten seconds, twelve every fifteen seconds. Try one minute's worth. You should do about forty-eight. Put everything out of your mind except that beer bottle and concentrate on the breathing by doing it rhythmically. You should get into a nice, easy pattern.

I guarantee you, a couple of sets of these will relax you. You'd be surprised how this simple breathing technique will enable you to hang in there until the train pulls into your station, or the elevator gets to your floor or the bus gets out of the tunnel and onto the ramp to Howard Johnson's. It does work.

There are a number of different breathing exercises which apply at various times of the labor/delivery process. What you have to do is learn all of them and then coach her. This means counting the exercises as she does them and making her concentrate on an object. This, my friends, is not easy to do. Why? Because it is not the exercises which are difficult, but taking the time to do them.

The Lamaze people call for a twenty-minute workout every day. Have you ever come home from a hard day's work and then had to go through twenty to thirty minutes of various exercises beginning with "Contraction begins.

Fifteen seconds, thirty seconds, forty-five seconds, one minute. Contraction ends" and on and on? It is a pain in the neck. All you want to do is watch a little TV. What is this nonsense with counting and breathing and clock-watching? You do that at the office. However, it's not really nonsense. It's all a part of being such a coach.

The problem, of course, that any coach has is maintaining his concentration and sanity. If you decide to try this natural method, you will have to handle the coaching chores in some acceptable way. I make one suggestion. Act like a real drillmaster. This is one of the few times that you will be able to get away with such a tactic. Be tough on her like Lombardi. Go get 'em. Remember, whatever you are doing, you are doing for all three of you. Get yourself a whistle and a stopwatch. If you really care about what you are doing, she will follow you 110 percent.

Face her and breathe with her throughout each contraction to help her maintain her concentration.

The manual calls for you to be forceful, to call out numbers and commands, to squeeze her leg to see if she is really concentrating (supposedly if she is, she won't feel your squeeze like she won't feel the contractions). Do it.

There's a lot more to this coaching stuff than meets the eye. What it really means is that you will have something important to do instead of just sitting around and whittling away on your cuticles. It makes you an integral part of the birth process, just as you were an integral part of the conception process.

In short, you become more of an expert than she does and as such, she turns to you for advice, support, and encouragement. Don't knock it. There is nothing wrong with this and when all the laughter dies down, you will be quite surprised at the extent of your participation in this entire procedure.

How good is it? Dr. Boris L. O'Mansky, a pediatrician with a busy private practice in the Baltimore area, says that the natural childbirth method is "encouragement for more bonding among the mother, the father and the child. That's one of the reasons for its popularity and the beauty of it all." I couldn't agree more.

Another part of the course I took gave me a tour of the hospital. It afforded me an opportunity to see what was really going on. I was trooped around to the admissions, labor, and delivery room and if there was ever a time I wanted to play doctor, this was it. You would be surprised how much attention is given to the male. I was handed a scrub suit, just like the doctors wear, with hat, shoes and all, and I was given access to just about everything that was going on; in short, I was treated as an *indispensable* part of this birth process. I even had dinner in the doctor's cafeteria.

One other aspect of this natural childbirth method should be mentioned: the "goody bag." This is nothing more than a brown paper bag which the mother-to-be is to bring to the hospital during the labor period. It is supposed to contain certain things to assist her. For example:

1. A picture to focus on during labor
2. Tape to hang the picture up
3. Washcloths
4. Mouthspray
5. Chap Stick

In other words, valuable items to enable her to ride through the labor period, which can be very long or very short. No food. No drinks. Now, when you get right down to it, the stuff I mentioned can easily be supplied by the hospital. What then is a goody bag? Who then is it for? Aha! One good guess. Here's what to take:

1. Make sure you have some sort of snack. She may not want you to leave the room and you may not want to leave. Therefore, have a bag of Hershey kisses available. They go a long way. Do not bring salami sandwiches. They can stink up the room and will only make her nauseous, which will then cause her to throw up, which will cause you to run out of the room and . . . well, you get the picture.
Hershey kisses are good. They dissolve in the mouth, last a relatively long time, and are sweet enough to fill you up quickly.

2. Do *not* bring anything which will get you drunk and possibly sick. If you can hold your beer, then bring a couple of bottles, but if you get tipsy when the foam comes out the top, then stay away.

3. Bring your stopwatch.

4. Bring a deck of cards. You may want to build houses with them.

5. Bring some interesting reading material, preferably action-adventure stories. This is no time to dwell on *Penthouse* or *Playboy* and certainly not *Hustler*.

6. Don't forget change for the telephone and a list of the numbers you want to call. Keep radios at home. It'll be just your luck that she'll decide to go into active labor at the top of the ninth, bases full.

7. Don't forget the camera. Actually, just fiddling around with it will make the time go that much faster.

So, what is the essence of this section? It comes down to this: Do you want to be involved in what's happening? There are some guys who want no part of it. Keep me away from the pain, the crying, the screaming, the blood. Okay, that's their prerogative, but nobody says it has to be that way. If you have a fear of being in the labor and delivery rooms, then you had best find out why, especially if you are still interested in this method of delivery. You also shouldn't be ashamed if you feel scared about the whole thing. It's not like going for a haircut.

I know that as far as I was concerned, I considered all aspects quite seriously. I mean, what if I screamed? What if I fainted? I spoke to a number of men who had gone through this technique and they were practically unanimous in their praise, stressing what a moving experience it was. None of them said they screamed and none of them fainted.

The fact is that you can limit the extent of your participation if you so desire. But the real answer is to decide what you want for yourself by exploring all the possibilities and by talking to as many people as possible. Those who do decide to participate will find themselves having what many fathers have called a "magnificent" experience. They get an in-depth feeling for the wife, the baby, and the whole delivery process.

One caveat. Stay away from talking to the generations before you. Remember, many procedures were quite different then. Talk to your contemporaries. Check with the hospital personnel, the obstetrician. Get an awareness of what is happening at the present time, not what happened in the past.

A noted obstetrician on Long Island, New York, Dr. Jerry A. Wider, says, "There is a tremendous emphasis on the natural method of delivery. In fact, it's almost overwhelming. Ten years ago, perhaps 5 to 10 percent of the couples considered natural childbirth. Today it's 60 percent. Those couples who have gone through natural have a closer relationship. They are sharing the experience from the beginning, experiencing the growth. The father is also brought into the mainstream much earlier. This is gratifying to me as an obstetrician to be able to treat a couple, rather than an individual."

Ah yes, I remember it well. Sitting up there on the mantle, sandwiched between my old Marine Corps fatigue cap and the ticket stubs from the Knicks/Lakers championship game, are my whistle and my stopwatch—remembrances of things past, but certainly not forgotten.

Obstetrical Terms

A "definition" is the action or process of stating a meaning. You will probably be seeing and hearing the same words over and over. Therefore, it wouldn't be a bad idea to understand what these words mean. The following, then, is a handy glossary of common obstetrical terms:

Afterbirth: The placenta and fetal membranes that are expelled after delivery.

Amniocentesis: A process whereby a sample of the amniotic fluid that surrounds the fetus in the uterus is withdrawn to determine whether any genetic disorders are apparent. It will also indicate the baby's sex. If interested, ask your doctor about it.

Analgesics: A drug such as Demerol which reduces pain, but which does not change the state of consciousness.

Anesthetics: A drug which relieves pain by numbing the area, or by rendering the patient unconscious. (NOTE: There is a difference between the two. Remember the section on methods of delivery?)

Apgar Test: Don't worry, it's not another exam left over from high school days. Actually, it's the child's first test (they start them early) and it is an evaluation of the infant during the first few minutes after birth. The score is determined by certain factors, such as the infant's color, muscle tone, heart rate, and cry.

Bag of Waters: Simply, it is the membrane containing amniotic fluid which surrounds the baby in the uterus.

Bloody Show: Blood-tinged mucus from the cervical opening which is expelled before and during labor.

Braxton-Hicks Contractions: These are intermittent, painless contractions of the uterus toward the end of pregnancy. Sort of practice contractions.

Breech: It's where the baby is coming out bottom or feet first.

Caesarean Section: Also called a "section," it is the delivery of the baby by incision through the abdominal wall and the wall of the uterus.

Caput: Appearance of the baby's head at the vaginal opening. It is also known as sheer excitement, or "Get the hot water, quick."

Cervix: The lower portion or neck of the uterus.

Crowning: The appearance of the *largest* part of the baby's head at the vaginal opening. It is otherwise defined as, "Hurry up with that hot water."

Demerol: An analgesic administered by injection during labor to aid in relaxation and to help reduce pain. It is probably one of the most well-known drugs around today.

Dilation: She's five fingers dilated. She's six fingers dilated. She's seven. She's fully dilated. Dilation is the widening of the cervical opening to permit the baby's head to pass through. Ten centimeters means fully dilated. It also means, "Here comes the baby."

Dipping: When the baby's head is between floating and engagement. See *Engagement.*

E.D.C.: Expected date of confinement. Why confinement? That means birth. Don't use this definition in front of her. Say Due Date. She'll go bananas over that word confinement.

Effacement: This is the gradual thinning-out of the cervix before and during labor. You need a fully effaced and a fully dilated condition of the cervix for the baby to pop through. Yes, I agree that the cervix is a very busy fellow.

Engagement: It's when the largest measurement of the baby's head descends into the pelvis. It takes place usually two to six weeks before the birth. In other words, the baby gets locked into position awaiting blast-off time.

Epidural: This refers to an anesthetic which numbs the body from the waist down.

Episiotomy: A surgical incision of the perineum (that portion of skin between the anus and the vagina) which enlarges the vaginal opening to expedite the birth and to preserve the tissues. That's where you hear the term "stitches."

F.H.R.: An easy one. Fetal heart rate. It's usually 120 to 160 beats per minute before birth. That's the baby I'm talking about. Yours will be like a drum roll by Buddy Rich.

Floating: The position of the baby in the uterus before its head reaches the engagement stage.

Forceps: As we discussed before, it is an instrument used to aid in the delivery of the baby's head.

Fundus: It's the upper portion of the uterus, just in case you hear somebody mention it.

Induction: The initiation of labor through artificial means, usually with the administration of a drug called Pitocin.

Monitor: A machine which is used to observe the baby's heartbeat and the uterine contractions. Its purpose is to make sure everything is functioning properly. A marvelous machine.

123

Mucous Plug: A plug of mucus which blocks the cervix during pregnancy. When it is expelled, it is referred to as the bloody show. What do you mean you just had lunch?

Occiput Posterior: It's when the back of the baby's head presses against the mother's spine, causing back labor.

Pelvic Floor: A sling of muscles which supports the pelvic organs and through which the baby must pass during delivery. Three cheers for the pelvic floor!

Pelvimetry: An x-ray evaluation of the pelvis to determine its capacity for delivery.

Perineum: The region between the vagina and the rectum where the episiotomy is made at the time of delivery.

Phases of Labor: The differences in contractions at labor time. *Phase One* means "early," *Phase Two* means "active," and *Phase Three* means "transition." (This will be discussed in greater detail toward the end of this book.)

Pitocin: The hormone which is given either intravenously or by placing a small, flat pill under the tongue. Its function is to induce or speed up labor.

Placenta: A circular, vascular structure which nourishes the baby throughout pregnancy. It is attached to the upper portion of the uterus or fundus, and is expelled following the baby's birth. It then becomes the afterbirth.

Premature Labor: The onset of labor after only twenty-eight weeks of pregnancy, but before the full maturity of the baby. A premature baby would follow, usually one born in about the seventh month of pregnancy.

Quickening: The first time the mother feels the baby move.

Sonogram: A specific medical test. It offers an outline of the anatomic structures through the use of ultrasound. The reason? It determines the size of the baby and the position of the placenta.

Sphincter: A muscle surrounding and closing an opening.

Stages of Labor: Not quite a definition, but you should know what they are. *First Stage*: From the onset of labor to complete dilation of the cervix. Complete dilation is ten centimeters. *Second Stage*: From dilation through the birth of the baby. *Third Stage*: Expulsion of the placenta.
Station: This is the measurement of the descent of the baby through the birth canal during labor.
Transition: Usually the last two centimeters of cervical dilation before the pushing begins. It is Phase Three of the First Stage of Labor, and it's a rough one.
Vernix: The cheeselike material which covers the skin of the baby in the uterus.
Vertex: The presenting part of the baby or head, true in 95 percent of all labors.

Memorize these terms and then pick up your medical license at the hot dog stand on the corner.

Genetics
Go up to a pregnant woman. "Let me see your hands," you say. If she holds her hands out with the palms up, the baby will be a boy. If palms are down, it's a girl. This technique comes from Eastern Europe and most of the people in that area of the world will swear by it, notwithstanding the fact that you may categorize the belief as another old wives' tale.

There is also a recent ritual which is used considerably in Western Civilization, although it is not classified the same way. It is the Ring-on-a-String test. Some people claim that its results are uncannily accurate. Apparently, say these same people, the body is capable of emitting certain vibrations, wavelengths if you will, expressing the internal condition of an individual. What exponents of this view feel is that the woman *really* knows whether she is carrying a boy or a girl. After all, the baby is a part of her and if anyone is sure of what's going on, she would be.

The Ring-on-a-String procedure is quite simple. The woman lies flat on her back. Her wedding ring is removed from her finger and is looped by a piece of string. You dangle the ring about six inches above her stomach. Once the ring has stopped moving and the woman is totally relaxed, you ask her a series of basic questions.

For example:

"Are you pregnant? Is your name _____? Do you have two arms? Do you have four legs?"

The answers to these questions will give off specific vibrations which will cause the ring to move, either in a circular motion or in a back-and-forth motion. The particular answer establishes a "yes" or "no" response to the question asked. If she answers "yes" to the question "Are you pregnant?" and the ring moves in a circle, but a "yes" response to the question "Do you have four legs?" produces a back-and-forth motion of the ring, then you have established a common denominator: A circular swing evidences a truthful answer while a lie results in the other movement. Of course, there is always the possibility that . . .

However, once the pattern is set, then you can go on with other questions, leading up to the ultimate one: "Is there a boy in you?" or "Is the baby a girl?" Naturally, if you get past this part, you can try and probe even more as to what the baby will look like, but let me save you some time. Besides, that's what this section is about.

There is a plethora of written material available on the physical characteristics of your baby, as well as its sex. These materials may be found in any library or they can be obtained from almost any obstetrician's office, or they will be sent to you by nearly all the baby-food companies. All you have to do is fill out one of those slips in any baby furniture store—you know, the one which is also having a perpetual contest whereby you can win ten million dollars if you're lucky enough to have your name picked "at random." The contest has been going on for as long as I care to remember and I have yet to know when this at-random selection will be made.

At any rate, fill out one of those cards and in short order you will be bombarded with all kinds of literature, including, without limitation, genetic determinations.

The books will tell you what kind of baby you will have and what your baby will look like. Supposedly, these tomes are based on years and years of study; by whom, they don't say.

When we talk about genetic determinations, we are talking about an area which, to many people, is colored not only by more of the old wives' tales, but by a lot of unnecessary folderol. Genetics is the biology of heredity, particularly the study of hereditary transmission and variation. Heredity, so that we don't lose anybody here, is the sum total of the qualities and potentialities derived from one's ancestors.

This pretty much accounts for why you look the way you do. Now, understand that sex determination really doesn't come under this genetic banner. The baby will be either a boy or a girl, depending on the meeting of a particular sperm and the egg. This means that the mother's egg has nothing to do with it. The father ejaculates two types of spermatozoa in apparently equal numbers. Thus, the sex of the child is purely a matter of chance. There is not much you can do about this.

Although sex is determined at the moment of fertilization, there has been some study on whether the two types of sperm are always produced in such equal proportions. There have been a number of opinions on this aspect to the effect that if you have intercourse during a certain time of the fertile period and in a certain way, the chances are greater that you will have one gender rather than the other. So, if you are interested in having a boy more than a girl, you might want to explore this further.

There are other interesting theories supposedly controlling what the sex of the baby will be, some dealing with what you eat, what you drink, the position of the moon, and countless other machinations, all calculated to keep you in a constant state of confusion. The fact remains that because your mother had five sons and *her* mother had six sons will be no indication that yours will definitely be a boy. Sure, if you want to take odds on its being a male, you can get pretty good takers, but you will still have the same fifty-fifty shot as anybody else.

The same concept also applies to twins, but in this instance percentages play an important part. If, for example, this is your first child and your wife is thirty years of age, then statistics show that for every 1,000 births, there will be twelve involving twins. If, on the other hand, your wife is forty years old and this is your fourth child, then you will find twenty-one births involving twins for every 1,000. The chances of having multiple births generally increase as the age and number of children increase.

Therefore, if you've been hoping for a boy, be prepared also for a girl. The chances are just that: one out of two, and, as I said before, there is really nothing you can do about it.

There is a procedure now being used which can tell you your baby's sex. Amniocentesis, a procedure which is used in discovering whether there is any genetic disorder, will also tell you the sex of the unborn child. A thin, hollow needle is inserted through the abdominal wall and into the uterus, and a small amount of the amniotic fluid which surrounds the fetus is withdrawn to be tested.

We have all been exposed to the incredible variations on the subject of genetics. Take a family of three boys, for example. You might find the oldest resembling both the father and mother, the second son resembling some aunt in Florida, and the third one looking like the mailman.

Even within the same family, there is no telling who belongs to who. For instance, if you have brown eyes and the mother of your child has blue eyes, then there is a fifty-fifty chance the child will also have brown eyes. This is quite scientific, for as the engineers in the audience can readily see, this means too that there is a fifty-fifty chance the kid will have blue eyes.

For the most part, however, the following pattern will govern (at least with respect to eyes):

Blue eyes are the most predictable. Thus, if both parents have blue eyes, you can pretty much bet next to your last dollar that the baby will also sport the same color peepers. By the same token, two brown-eyed parents will probably yield a brown-eyed child (but not always).

If there is one and one in the family (mother's eyes brown, father's eyes blue), then there is a 50/50 chance the eyes of the baby will be brown or a lighter color. In such an eventuality, you might want to note that if the offspring is a female, she will most likely have darker eyes than if she were a he. Why? Because a woman's eyes are usually darker than a man's. Accordingly, research (see Amram Scheinfeld's *Your Heredity and Environment*, Lippincott, 1972) has shown that there are more blue-eyed males than blue-eyed females.

The Expectant Father's Survival Kit

I have compiled a chart at the end of this section with information derived from eminent obstetricians and geneticists. It will give you a pretty good indication of what you can expect. It is designed primarily to tell you what your child will *probably* look like, after taking into consideration what you and your lady look like.

But let me give you some pointers and background in order for you to make the best estimate of your child's characteristics. Let me tell you something about myself.

The Eyes

I have brown eyes. Not just brown eyes, but beady brown eyes which mostly peer through slits of eyelashes. They are beady brown eyes which were handed down from my father, who also has beady brown eyes from his father who had beady brown eyes too, and which apparently must have been all the rage in Kiev before the revolution. No wonder they deserted the Czar and came here. With all those millions of beady brown eyes, what could you expect but an insurrection.

Now my wife has blue eyes. Oh, not just plain blue eyes, but big blue eyes. They are the kind which she uses to utmost advantage in job interviews and in exchanging merchandise in department stores. They work wonders. They do not come from Kiev. These are the same eyes which are found in County Cork and which you have seen on television surrounded by Maybelline.

With this combination, what would you say my kid will be like? You're right. Let's hope for the best.

The Nose

All babies save those born of kangaroos have cute little button noses which generally last from the delivery room until the date of first visitation from friends, especially the beautiful-people friends.

Some noses are flat, some are wide, some are squished, some are squashed. For a personal note, my nose is long. Yes, that long. It also has a small bump which somebody years ago was supposed to have corrected. Something about a deviated septum. I never did follow through.

Size? Well, with ruler in hand, I measure two and three-fourths inches from stem to stern. Something to sneeze about, to be sure. The wife has a slightly smaller nose. What would you expect with blue eyes from the Old Sod, Pinocchio's mother? According to the books, my child has a fifty-fifty shot at coming forth with a proboscis of noteworthy dimensions.

The Mouth

Most babies have tiny rosebud mouths. I have a fairly full one with decent lips; so does my wife. Mouths don't bother me that much. After all, how many people do you know who go around saying, "That Charlie, what a lousy mouth he has." This is quite different from, "Boy does he have a foul mouth."

The chart at the end of this section will give you some indication of what to expect.

The Head

A high forehead usually means intelligence. A low forehead usually means hair. Mine, since you ask, is high. So high, in fact, that it extends well into the middle of my head. That's where the skin stops and the hair starts. The distaff side? Low. A low forehead. Prognosis for the baby? He/she will either look very intelligent or very weird.

131

The Hair

While we're on the subject of headbones, let's take a look at hair coloring. Some interesting sidelights apply here. Blonde hair produces blonde hair. A combination of blondes and brunettes tends to produce brunettes. Sometimes they also produce blondes; rarely do they turn out redheads. Redheads, though, produce not only redheads but also both blondes and brunettes although the brunettes are generally light brown.

The color of hair changes rather quickly with babies and you will probably have no idea what your child's official hair color will be until he or she is halfway through the sixth grade. A baby's hair is either there at birth, or there is none. It falls out when it wants to, grows back when it wants to, and changes so many times you may think you sired a chameleon. If you have dark hair, as I do, and the lady has light hair, like mine does, then the chances are the baby will have dark hair. That's one-half of the time. Guess what the other one-half is?

The Height, Weight, Build

Do whatever you want, eat whatever you want, exercise all you want, a child's basic height and weight has already been determined at the moment of fertilization. If it is destined that you will have a seven-footer, then that's what you will get. Not necessarily at birth, mind you, but there is nothing you will be able to do about height.

Weight is another matter. You could give birth to a child who will have a natural propensity to be heavy. That's where diet will enter the picture. You could also have a child with a tendency toward slenderness. For your information, boys are usually a few ounces heavier than girls at birth.

132

Months 7, 8, & 9

Genetics also seems to have some part in determining whether your baby will be naturally left-handed or naturally right-handed. Also, genetics will determine whether she or he will have ten toes or eleven, and, to some extent, what kind of disposition the baby may possess.

If you add up the figures on the chart, you should get a rather good reading of what to expect, although I guarantee you it will never come out precisely that way. Remember, the genes within both you and the mother-to-be represent a combination of your respective ancestors; thus, it's quite possible that your offspring might just resemble some great-uncle.

As for me, our baby should have a high forehead, not too much hair, brown eyes (which are slightly on the beady side), a prominent nose, full apple cheeks, and an interesting mouth. Height and weight? Well, from a slim six-foot frame and a solid 5'2" body, it's anyone's guess. From bologna legs to spindles, from broad shoulders to no hips, you can take your pick.

What can I look for, then? I don't really know, but one thing is certain: The baby better have a good personality!

EYE COLOR

Parents	Child
Both dark	Dark
Both light	Light
One dark, one light	50/50 dark or light

HAIR COLOR

Both black	Black
One black, one light	50/50 black or light

The Expectant Father's Survival Kit

Both brown	Brown
Both blonde	Blonde
Both red	Red, light-brown or blonde
One red, one blonde	50/50 for red
One red, one dark	Probably dark

HAIR FORM

Both curly	Curly
Both wavy	Wavy
Both straight	Straight
One curly, one wavy	Curly
One wavy, one straight	Wavy

NOTE: Genes for frizzy or curly types tend to dominate straight hair. Curly dominates wavy; wavy dominates straight.

SKIN COLOR

Both white	White
Both black	Black
One white, one black	Mulatto
One white, one with darkish skin (e.g., Arabians and Mediterranean peoples)	In-between shade

FRECKLES

Generally runs in families with inheritance by way of dominant gene. Transmission of freckling is especially likely when red hair is also present.

NOSE

Both having small, straight noses	Same type
Both having very different shapes	Extreme details usually dominate

As a rule, if both parents have the same type of nose, the child's will generally be the same. If, however, one parent has a nose with an outstanding characteristic, the child's nose will usually follow that parent.

MOUTH

Follows parents but difficult to ascertain. In cases of children born to white and Negro parents, the Negro lips tend to dominate.

CHIN

Usually follows parents but if there are different shapes, the child will tend toward a straight rather than a receding chin. Another tendency would be toward a wide rather than a pointed chin. Clefts are likely to be dominant in inheritance.

DIMPLES

If a parent has dimples, the child will most likely have them too.

SHAPE AND STRUCTURE

Both tall	Tall
Both short	Short

One tall, one short	Short
Both slender	Slender
Both obese	Obese
One slender, one obese	Fifty-fifty either way

NOTE: Given exactly the same stature genes, a male will grow about 6 percent taller than a female. There is a tendency, however, in recent generations for tallness; but shortness genes still dominate tallness genes.

SEX CHARACTERISTICS

Female arms are usually at an angle.
Male arms are straight.
Female legs are slightly knock-kneed.
Male legs are straight.

Sex

The eggs of the female all carry the X chromosome. The sperm of the male carry two kinds: half carry an X chromosome, half carry a Y. Thus, if an X sperm enters an egg, the XX combination results in a girl. If a sperm with a Y enters an egg, the XY combination results in a boy.

Twins are categorized as follows: Identical twins are those from the same single egg and a single sperm. They are the same sex. Fraternal twins are those from two different eggs, fertilized by two different sperms. And triplets . . .

So, do you have a preference?

"I want a boy to play baseball with."

"Girls are best. They're supposed to be easier, and besides they're cuter."

"A boy is my choice because then you don't have to put up with dresses, weddings, and dolls."

"Nope. Girls are sweeter and more cooperative."

"I don't know," says Ira Rosenberg of Brooklyn, New York. "If it's a girl, I hope it doesn't look like me. If a boy, okay, but boys are easy. Give them a truck and they're happy."

"Girls are better," says Charles Dodd of Amityville, Long Island. "They'll take what's in the truck."

Organizing the Home

As long as we are making determinations, there is one particular area which becomes crucial to you at this time: organizing the home. No snickering, please. This may wind up in your lap so you should know something about it.

During the woman's latter months, you will find that she may not be in the mood nor have that much energy to do what has to be done around the house. She is probably getting quite anxious as to what will be happening in a few weeks at the hospital. Therefore, you may be doing more at night than just reading the evening comics. One prospective father said, "My wife keeps buying stuff and I keep putting it together. Sometimes I don't know what some of the things are."

But a lot more than connecting leg A to slot B may be thrust on your burly shoulders. Accordingly, it would be best for you to have an idea of who's on first. Organizing is simply a matter of putting things in perspective and finding a logical format in which to operate.

There is included here a checklist of things to do. Simply rip these pages out and tack them onto the wall. As soon as an item is completed, check it off.

Now, let's break everything down into its basic parts:

137

Baby's Wardrobe

Undoubtedly, you will receive a number of items as gifts. Undoubtedly, you will receive a number of duplicate items as gifts. Undoubtedly, you will have too much of one particular article of clothing but not enough of something else. Consequently, you have to know what to keep and what to exchange. For example, if you live in Atlanta, a baby will not need fifteen blankets. Conversely, one blanket may not be enough if you are a resident of Anchorage.

Therefore, keep what you really will use and take back the rest for things you will require. Refunds are also acceptable. Aha, now you're interested, eh? A couple of tips on baby clothes: Don't buy too much of anything. Infants grow fast. You should get a minimum supply for maximum usage.

Also, look for those items which can be laundered easily. Don't get saddled with clothes which require ironing or dry cleaning. Machine washable and pre-shrunk garments are your best bets.

Baby's Toiletries

Check with your pediatrician as to what is preferred. For example, some doctors dislike the use of powder; others only recommend creams; some use neither. Whatever it is, try and buy in quantity. If there is a sale on cotton balls, and you know you will be using cotton balls, then stock up now. They certainly won't spoil.

Baby's Pediatrician

The final months of pregnancy are a perfect time to secure the services of a pediatrician. If anything, it takes the mother-to-be's mind off her own condition. As we discussed in the section on selecting an obstetrician, choose your baby's doctor the same way. Follow the procedure as you did with that selection, but this time put a great deal of emphasis on how close the pediatrician is to your home, policy regarding house calls, whether competent people cover for him or her *at all times,* and whether his or her ideas fit in with what you want for your child. In other words, what's the doctor's philosophy? Does it agree with yours?

It is always advisable to meet with a pediatrician first as you can then get a good (or bad) feeling as to how he functions. Don't forget for one moment that you are entrusting your child to a stranger's hands.

By the same token, the pediatrician should be aware of your involvement. Most understand that after the birth of the baby, the father can feel like an older child, that the baby is taking his place. This is known as sibling rivalry.

You should, as Dr. O'Mansky told me, "Understand what a baby is and what happens, the same as what the mother learns. There is no one correct way to raise a child, but you can eliminate confusion through open discussion with your wife and by touching base with your pediatrician when questions arise."

Dr. O'Mansky feels that the father "should be an integral part in the development of the child, that he has to demonstrate he is a parent just like the mother does. He also has to share and he should understand the normal development and growth of the baby, bearing in mind that if he doesn't have much to do with the child, this affects the normal relationship with the wife."

The fact is that fathers are actually becoming more involved. Dr. Seymour Musiker, a prominent pediatrician in Stony Brook, New York, says, "In the past two years there has been an increase in the number of fathers bringing children to my office, especially on Saturdays. Sometimes as many as half of the patients come in with only their fathers. There has been a slow but steady evolution of the participation of fathers and I think it's because they *want* to become involved." Isn't that confirmed by the fact that you are reading this book?

Baby's Nurse

Remember too to check into nurses if you want the services of one. Talk this over with your mate. Do you really want a nurse? Can you afford one? Are you making plans to stay home for the first week the baby's home?

Now, this doesn't mean you have to employ a nurse, but if you want to, you should know where to find one. In this respect, there are a number of sources: (a) your obstetrician, (b) your pediatrician, (c) the hospital, (d) recommendations by friends, and (e) nursing services which are listed in the telephone book.

Whatever you decide, do it early. Three months before the baby arrives is certainly not too early.

The reason for having a nurse is primarily twofold: to give a new mother an opportunity to recoup her strength and to afford her access to information on baby care at a first-hand basis.

Again, no one says you must have a nurse. It is strictly a matter of preference.

Baby's Furniture and Room

Unless certain superstitions prevent you from doing so, it is always best to obtain the furniture and other equipment well in advance. Have it set up and ready to use. Don't be afraid to decorate the room. The days of stark white walls are gone and most psychologists and psychiatrists believe it is best to offer the newborn some visual stimulation. Red and yellow are the recommended colors. Remember, contrary to old wives' tales, a baby *does* see at birth. Also, if you need larger quarters, start acquiring them early. Don't wait until your wife enters her ninth month to make a move. It can be most unsettling, to say the least.

Money

As you can gather by now, all of the above requires money. By this time, you should have figured out where the money is coming from. Is she going back to work? If so, when? What happens if she decides later she doesn't want to, or does but not on a full-time basis? All of this should be discussed well in advance, if at all possible. Whatever plans you make, get them resolved before the final month.

Route to Hospital

It's exactly what it says. Prepare the route you will be taking so that you know where you are going and how. The last thing you need when the water breaks is to spend valuable time searching for the hospital's address in the telephone book or calling AAA for directions. Don't laugh. It has happened.

Safety at Home

It is not enough to decorate the baby's room and then call it quits. Before you know it, a week-old baby becomes a six-month-old baby, and before you have a chance to turn around, your child may be crawling along the kitchen floor rolling a can of Drano.

Therefore, take the necessary precautions before your baby comes home.

The Expectant Father's Survival Kit

1. Lock all medications and chemicals in a cabinet outside the baby's reach.

2. Remove all cleaning items from underneath sinks; place them high out of reach of children.

3. Block unused electrical outlets with dummy plugs.

4. Keep all important emergency numbers next to the telephone: pediatrician, police, fire, poison control center, nearest neighbor.

5. Take stock of what you have on tables. Some things will have to be removed.

6. See what furniture has sharp edges. Tape those edges.

Don't be sorry, be safe.

One final thought. What do you bring to the hospital for taking the baby home? Six things: a nightgown, an undershirt, a receiving blanket, a heavier blanket, a sweater, and a cap. That should do it.

CHECKLIST

Wardrobe and miscellaneous
6 undershirts, 3–6-months size   ———
4 nightgowns or kimonos, 6-months size ———
4 stretch suits, same size   ———
2 sweater sets   ———
4 washcloths   ———
2 towels (soft, terrycloth)   ———
2 crib mattress protectors   ———
3 crib sheets (form-fitted, noniron) ———
4 receiving blankets   ———
2 heavy blankets (1 thermal)   ———

Diapers
If you're using a diaper service, then you need at least a supply of one hundred birdseye diapers a week ⎯⎯
If you're using disposable diapers, you will probably use at lease sixty a week ⎯⎯

Toiletries
2 bags of triple-size cotton balls ⎯⎯
Baby safety scissors ⎯⎯
Double-lock safety pins (if regular diapers used) ⎯⎯
Talcum powder ⎯⎯
Baby lotion ⎯⎯
Baby soap ⎯⎯
Pacifier (recommend Nuk brand) ⎯⎯
Feeding supplies (check your pediatrician. If your wife is breast-feeding, forget this area) ⎯⎯

Furniture
Crib with firm mattress ⎯⎯
Bumpers (no pillows) ⎯⎯
Dressing table ⎯⎯
Toys, mobiles, decorations ⎯⎯

Suggested gifts
Humidifier ⎯⎯
Carrier (Snugli recommended) ⎯⎯
Infant seat (Bouncinette recommended) ⎯⎯
Stroller ⎯⎯
Playpen (starting at three months) ⎯⎯

143

Highchair (starting at six months) _____
Walker (starting at five months) _____
Car seat (starting at six months) _____

Additional
Secure pediatrician _____
Secure nurse (if applicable) _____
Revise your will _____
Check on insurance; change beneficiaries _____
Announcement cards _____
Reading material _____

With respect to that last item, you might want to take note of the following:

1. The premier baby book of all is still *Baby and Child Care*, by Dr. Benjamin Spock. Pocket Books publishes it and if you decide to get a copy, make sure it is the revised edition. It is all-encompassing and despite the backbiting by authors of other baby books, it is by far the most complete one on the market.

2. *The First Twelve Months of Life*, by the Princeton Center for Infancy and Early Childhood, is fascinating. It is published by Grosset & Dunlap and is an account, in text, pictures, and charts, of a baby's growth month by month. Excellent.

3. A rather different kind of book is Marvin J. Gersh's *How to Raise Children at Home in Your Spare Time*. It is published by Stein and Day and is not your usual baby book. Dr. Gersh is a pediatrician who has taken the time to narrow the problems down into what's serious and what's not and why. He's also not taken himself too seriously and,

as a result, it's the most amusing book I've read on the subject.

Of course, if reading is not your forte, you might want to consider attending a class on baby care. Classes for expectant parents are sponsored by various organizations including hospitals, the Red Cross, nursing associations, health care groups, and religious centers. Check around. It's well worth your time.

A Special Report from the Inside—Ninth Month

Uterus has dropped down into the pelvis and is ready for the delivery of the baby. Contractions begin as the cervix dilates to enable the baby to pass into the birth canal. The woman begins to feel spasmodic contractions. The abdomen hardens. The baby is fully developed. It is separated from the outside world by approximately four inches. The countdown begins.

Labor: At the Hospital

Okay, fellows, we are now at the zero hour. At one point, in or around the ninth month, it will all stop. It will just go away; that is, all the bumping and grinding and hopping. You will then probably find that your ship is holding liquid, too much liquid. You will awake one night (everything takes place at night or early morning) and you will need a bucket to bail you out. The water has broken.

Now, before you turn green and begin to get the shakes, you should know what you can expect when labor begins so that you know what you are dealing with. Labor starts in many ways. First of all, understand what it is. Labor is the activity of the uterus in its function of moving the baby down and out. One word of caution: What is being set forth here doesn't always happen in exactly the same way for everybody. Each labor is different; however, the following is the *usual* way it happens.

Engagement (the baby's head locked in the pelvic area) takes place anywhere from two to six weeks before the onset of labor. She will return from a visit to the obstetrician and tell you of this. That will be tip-off number one. Then, the mother-to-be will experience a surge in her activity. She may have more energy then ever before. She might go on a cleaning, scrubbing, dusting, and polishing binge. That is tip-off number two that labor may be but a few days away. She may also undergo some small contractions (Braxton-Hicks) with increased vaginal discharge. More hints that your child is en route.

In the first phase of labor, the cervix begins to dilate (usually up to three centimeters) and contractions are mild. They will last anywhere from thirty seconds to a minute and occur at irregular intervals, say from five to twenty minutes apart. This is considered the longest part of labor. Why? Because it may go on for five hours or more.

Here is where you can't lose your cool. Unless the hospital is hours away, there is no reason to rush everybody into the car. Your mate may want to go to the hospital for fear the baby will pop out on the living room rug, but this will not happen. Help her remain calm. Keep an eye on the contractions, time their frequency and length, but most importantly, try to distract her as best you can. How? Take her to a movie. Play cards with her. Watch television. Give her a shower.

As far as you are concerned, get yourself ready. If you're hungry, eat something. You probably won't have a chance or feel like it later on. Do you feed her? Generally, she is not to eat anything. She could have ginger ale or tea or even a drink, but call the doctor first and ask him for specific instructions. This is the early phase of labor and you can expect it to last about five hours, some less, some more.

The second phase is what is known as active labor. The cervix continues to dilate (to about eight centimeters) and the contractions are much stronger. Now they last for about a minute and come every three minutes or so.

At this point, she will experience pressure over the pubic bone and perhaps an ache in the lower portion of her back. She will be extremely nervous and increasingly dependent on you. To say she will be scared would be an understatement.

By this time, you will probably be on your way to the hospital. Don't forget to bring with you any necessary insurance cards, all hospital forms or receipts, telephone numbers, and a supply of change—and, of course, the mother-to-be.

Your function during this period is to give her reassurance and encouragement. Try to keep her as relaxed as possible. If you are using the Lamaze Method, you will know about the breathing techniques. Get to work on them immediately. Also, this is the time to put that goody bag to use. Pop a few Hershey kisses into your mouth. Crack open a can of beer. Sit next to her and keep her forehead and lips moist with a cool, damp washcloth. She may get a little off-the-wall so it will not be easy to distract her. That's okay. Just be prepared to keep her as comfortable as you can. Expect this stage to last for a few hours.

We now enter the third phase known as the transition period. This is where it hits the fan. The cervix is dilating the last few centimeters. The contractions are very strong.

They may last a minute and a half and seem to come one on top of another. This is by far the most difficult part of labor. She will be noticeably irritable and may not be coherent. Disregard whatever she may say to you of a detrimental nature, including, without limitation, "I hate you. Go to hell. You're responsible for this." And, of course, "I'm going to Tahiti." She's being overwhelmed by pressure and she will be absolutely terrified.

Okay, Harold, here's where your coaching, your coolness, and your support come under close scrutiny. Don't leave her alone even for an instant. Keep encouraging and reassuring her that what she is experiencing is perfectly normal. Continue to be strong and give her guidance. This period lasts for around an hour and after that it will be all over. The doctor will say "cervix fully dilated" and he will begin advising her when and when not to push.

At this juncture, if you are going into the delivery room, you will be taken to the scrub room and outfitted in the proper attire. And then, you will be off to Delivery for the next stage of fatherhood.

Delivery: By Yourself

Hold everything! Wait a minute! I missed something. What happens if you are in the boondocks and she goes into labor and the contractions are two minutes apart and your car has a flat tire (two flat tires) and you're trapped inside the log cabin by a snow storm and the baby will arrive in thirty minutes and the nearest doctor is forty minutes away?

Well, as strange as it sounds, don't panic. Remember, birth is a natural process. The baby usually will get born despite everyone or anything: It's been this way for thousands of years. Keep calm. Send for medical help and in the meantime, follow this simple procedure. Ready, Freddy? No fancy tricks now. It's show time!

1. Have something to put the baby in. It can be a box, a drawer, a towel, even unread newspapers (they're cleaner).

2. Have a pair of scissors at the ready. Sterilize them in boiling water for at least ten minutes.

3. Have some clean string or cord (even shoelaces) by your side. You need two pieces, each at least ten inches in length.

4. Scrub your hands well. Put some kind of clean hanky over your mouth and nose to serve as a mask.

5. Have the mother-to-be lie with knees up toward her body.

6. You will see something black in the opening of the vagina. That's the baby's head.

7. Do not have her force the baby out too rapidly. Slow and easy on the pushing. Her mouth should be open and she should pant during contractions. Keep the air coming in.

8. When the widest part of the head has come out, support it with your hands. The back of the head will probably be toward you.

9. The shoulders follow quickly, but make sure they come out one at a time. No need to hurry. Slow and easy. Put your hands under the baby's armpits and lift. Again, no forcing.

10. The umbilical cord will still be attached. *Note*: *Never, never pull that cord*. If it is wrapped around the baby's neck, then gently ease it away.

11. The baby will be wet and slippery; thus, the need for a towel so you can hold the infant easily.

12. The baby should cry as soon as the head emerges. If not, hold the baby upside down. No need to slap the

149

back. It'll cry. A flick on the soles of the feet will also do. Make sure the baby's mouth has no mucous inside. Just put a finger in and get the mucous out.

13. Cover the baby up. Keep it warm.

At this point, the doctor should be pounding on your door. If not, the next order of business is the cord.

14. Put the baby on the mother's stomach. Let her hold it. The afterbirth should come out within ten minutes.

15. Now, take one length of string and tie it tightly around the cord, about six inches from the baby's stomach. Not too tightly, mind you. Don't cut into the cord. Take the other length of string and tie it in the same way, but six inches further down the cord; in other words, twelve inches from the baby's stomach.

16. Wait until the cord *between* the tied strings stops pulsating and then cut through it with the scissors. It is an easy cut.

17. The afterbirth? Don't worry. It slides out by itself and you can just cover it over with newspapers. You won't mind. You'll be so busy and excited anyway at everything around you that you won't really notice what's been coming out of her.

My friend, you are finished. Now you can go to the front door and let the doctor in. You should have a big smile on your face and, I daresay, some tears in your eyes.

B-Day

There is only one way to understand fully what it is like to have a baby and that is to experience it firsthand. For the woman, birth may have one meaning; for us men, it may be something entirely different.

"Maureen prepared dinner on Sunday night, but she

wasn't very hungry. She went into the bedroom to lie down. She had been getting various contractions all day and when the contractions got stronger, I called the doctor. We started out for the hospital. I was driving slowly, carefully, trying to restrain the tenseness I was starting to feel. When we reached the hospital, Maureen was four centimeters dilated. I went with her into the labor room, although I began to wonder what I was doing there. I applied wet towels to her face. She said it was fantastic. Maybe that's what I'm doing there. At 12:20 A.M., she was wheeled into the delivery room. I guess I just went with her. It seemed silly to sit in a chair in an empty room. The baby was born at 12:47. I have to admit I was fine throughout except I do remember once calling a temporary halt to the proceedings so that I could reload my camera. Maureen nearly strangled me. The problem was I got so excited during the actual delivery that I missed taking some pictures. What can I tell you? It was the most incredible thing that has ever happened to me. I couldn't possibly ever forget it. Afterwards, we were both starved and I went out and brought in French toast with lots of syrup. We gobbled it down sitting on the hospital bed at two in the morning. Yeah, the two of us gobbled it down, the third member was sleeping."

—The birth of David Sean
Rosenberg, June 20, 1977
New York City

"That's what really got me. Two of us went into that hospital and three of us came out."

—Ron (San Francisco)

"I stayed downstairs in the waiting room. You see, I have this thing about being around anything medical. I get very

151

The Expectant Father's Survival Kit

squeamish. I let the doctor tell me. And even then I almost
passed out."

—Anonymous (Paramus, N.J.)

"I thought natural would be the best way. It was for a
time, but after twenty-five hours I thought it would never
end. I began to feel helpless. I think it's great if the labor is
a short one, but—"

—Alan S. (San Diego)

"This is my fifth kid. They call me at Mike's place. That's
a bar. This way, I can celebrate right at the moment and I
do. You want a free beer? Catch me at Mike's on delivery
date."

—Alan T. (Chicago)

Yours could be like these or, perhaps, it will be like
mine.

It was 1:10 A.M., Monday, October 27, when it started.
Coincidentally, it was also my parents' Fortieth Wedding
Anniversary. We didn't plan it that way. Actually, we ex-
pected the baby in November.

We had just finished watching a mystery movie and the
11 o'clock news. Sunday nights were always difficult to get
to sleep early. When you have no children Sunday is a day
for sleeping: arise late for brunch, watch a few ball games
on TV, take some naps. By the time bedtime rolls around,
you know it's going to be rather hard trying to get a good
night's sleep, especially when the following day is the start
of another work week.

But, for some reason which I didn't realize at the time,
this particular Sunday night was more restless than usual.
We had also spent some of the day practicing the breathing
exercises, trying to decide on the baby's name, and still

wondering what gift we could give for the anniversary, although deep down I guess we both knew what would be the perfect one.

As I said, it was an uneasy night. The traffic outside the window seemed to agree: horns blew, tires screeched, people argued, dogs barked. The clock had struck twelve some thirty minutes ago as I continued to stare at the shadows of the cars and buses traversing the ceiling. I tried to think of the basketball game I had seen on television that afternoon, but one dunk shot kept replaying itself and I couldn't get it out of my mind. Sort of like what happens when you are constantly being interrupted while reading and you find yourself going over the same line time and time again.

I had just closed my eyes when a beam of light from the bathroom forced them open.

"Nancy, any problem?"

No answer.

"Nance, everything okay?"

She came out and sat down on the edge of the bed. She was pale. Her arms quivered.

"I don't know. I'm all wet."

She tried to smile.

"Wet?" I looked down and saw that her side of the bed was sopping and that there was a trail of fluid running along the floor to the bathroom.

"I think my water broke," she said.

I immediately picked up on the word "think." She wasn't sure. Well, how could she be sure? It was her first baby and what would she know from water breaking? For that matter, what would I know either?

"Okay," I tried to say as calmly as possible, switching on the bedroom light at the same time. "Do you have any contractions?"

She nodded.

153

"Okay," I repeated. "Let's relax." I took a deep breath. "There's plenty of time to get to the hospital after the water breaks. At least twelve hours. So, there's no rush. Now, first order of business, let's turn up the heat; it's cold in here. Second, you sit still and tell me when the contractions begin and when they end and when they begin again."

I reached for my stopwatch.

"Third, we stay calm and don't worry. I'll call the doctor. Ah—where do we keep the phone?"

After timing the contractions, I called the doctor and apologized for waking him and I explained that the water had apparently broken and the contractions were eight minutes apart and . . .

He told us to go back to sleep and call him at breakfast time. In another hour the contractions were six minutes apart. I called him again, apologized, and told him it seemed like it was now breakfast time. He reiterated his suggestion: "Go back to sleep."

Taking this recommendation in the spirit and knowledge in which it was made, we proceeded to the living room, turning on all the lights in the apartment as we did. After an hour of general discussion punctuated by five-minute breaks of silence, the contractions had dropped to four minutes apart.

"I want to go to the hospital," she said. I reached for the phone. "All right," the voice on the other end reassured me. "Everything is okay. You have plenty of time. Go to the hospital. I'll meet you there in a half hour."

Within ninety seconds we were out the door hailing a cab and ten minutes later we were pulling up in front of Emergency. A wheelchair and an attendant were waiting for us. The doctor had already called the hospital.

Nancy was taken upstairs and I was ushered into the

admissions office to sign forms. A few minutes later, I was sitting on a wooden bench in the anteroom watching a porter buff the floor. It all seemed like something out of a movie, the same movies I criticized: late night/early morning, a race through the empty streets, the Emergency entrance, the floors being buffed. All quiet and still. No one around. The ideal time, it seemed, to have a baby—a time of day when everything was unreal for no one was seen and nothing moved. Even the street lights didn't work. They blinked a constant yellow.

I was beginning to drift off when a shoe nudged one of mine. The doctor greeted me with a smile and told me to follow him. We walked in silence through the dark, cool corridors until we came to a set of swinging doors with the words "Labor Rooms" printed, one word to each door. We entered a small corridor painted in a soft green.

I was given a white, full-length coat to put on and then went into room number three. There was a bed, an easy chair, a table, a light, a washstand. The room overlooked the river and was painted in a bright yellow. The large Westclox on the wall now registered three o'clock.

In a few minutes, Nancy came in. We seemed to be the only people on the floor except for three nurses and one doctor in residency. Our own doctor had already assured us that the birth would not be for another six hours and that he was going to get some sleep to be fresh for the delivery. That seemed logical.

I settled down in the easy chair and tried to make conversation. Nancy was studying the ceiling. Her legs were shaking. I tried to take her mind off this, but she was having none of that tactic. She was concentrating on what was happening to her. She said she was getting sporadic contractions but that they didn't hurt. She was anxious as to what would follow.

I started to talk about the names again. We had previously decided on using her maiden name as the baby's middle one for her mother, who had died a few months earlier. For a first name we were still debating between Billy (William) for my grandfather and David (which we liked) if a boy, and Kelly if a girl.

I was successful in taking her mind off the contractions for about a half-hour. But when they became more frequent, I went to the nursing station for help. She was offered medication, but refused it. She was as determined as ever to have a natural childbirth and was adamant about any kind of drug which in any way might wind up in the bloodstream of her baby.

They brought in a fetal monitor to register the baby's heartbeat against the contractions. I put the picture we had brought up on the wall and we began the breathing techniques we had learned from the Lamaze classes. I watched the fetal monitor and told her when the contractions were beginning, how long they were lasting, and when they were ending. In this way she could coordinate the breathing patterns to the peak periods of the contractions.

While I did this, I kept giving her encouragement and confidence. In between, I applied cold compresses to her forehead and mouth. I now knew what it meant to be part of the childbirth process, at least to this point, for I was constantly busy and the hours, as many as they were, seemed to fly by.

The Hershey kisses were never eaten, the magazines were never opened, the camera remained unoperated, and when I last looked out the window, the sun was peeking over the river and the traffic began to move on the streets below. It all seemed appropriate to what was going on within the walls of this little yellow room.

It was now 8:30 A.M. and a new team of nurses took over. Our doctor returned. He was rested, clean-shaven, and fully awake. I felt that I was now turning *my* patient over to him. The changing of the guards, it seemed.

He examined her immediately. "Son of a gun, dilation full, effacement full. Good job." He smiled at me. I could only nod in return, but my chest puffed out.

He called for a midwife to assist. The time was drawing near. I thought about what I had learned in the classes and from the books. Fully dilated, fully effaced. What follows now is the pushing stage. Oh, my God, that's the last stage. You mean we have already gone through transition? I didn't quite remember it. Was it at five o'clock, at six, at seven? When? I do remember one period when her head sunk deep into the pillow and her back arched and I was constantly reassuring her and applying the compresses and holding her arms, but I heard not a sound, not so much as a whimper. It seemed to pass before I knew it. It could have gone on for an hour, I didn't know. In fact, the past five hours all seemed to blend, to meld together, but it was practically over and we had done it—and *I* had done it. I had really carried my share. My head felt as if it was full of bubbles. I stepped back and watched.

The midwife was in front of Nancy urging her to push. The doctor studied the monitor. I could see certain blips start as she pushed. After five continuous hours of watching that machine, I could understand every blip, every movement, every beat. I frowned and I started to say something, but the doctor was already marking certain portions of the tape with a crayon.

He shook his head and I gripped the handle on the door.

"Nancy," he whispered. "Nancy, stop pushing. Don't push unless I tell you." He looked at the clock. 9:15. We had been at this for the past forty-five minutes.

He continued. "We're going into delivery now. I don't see the baby's head as yet. You've pushed long enough. I'm going to use forceps to get it out of there."

I looked at her face. I could see what she was thinking and although she said nothing, I knew she was not going to come this far and not take it to the end. I moved to the edge of the bed. "Nancy, listen to the doctor, okay?" She nodded and smiled.

The doctor ordered everyone to the delivery room. I started to sit in the easy chair, but a nurse came in carrying a cap, gown, shoes, and mask. She gave them to me and I knew that the rest period was still some time away. Actually, as she helped me get into these unfamiliar clothes, I felt a second wind coming—or was it a third—or even a fourth?

I slung the camera over my shoulder and watched the two nurses wheel the bed out of the room. When they were gone, the doctor came over to me.

"I told her we were using forceps because the indications on the screen show that the umbilical cord was around the baby's neck and that each time she pushed, the cord tightened. Once I can see the head, I can reach in and relieve the neck from that cord."

He was clear, clean, unemotional.

I nodded my understanding and we started for the delivery room. This was a small room containing a scale, a warmer, some cabinets, and a large padded table under a huge light. The table faced a window and the sun streamed in, brightening and warming everything. A perfect room, a perfect day, a perfect day for . . . I held my breath.

158

I studied the doctors and nurses as they moved into their positions. I was offered a low stool next to Nancy. She was watching what was going on in the overhead mirror. Her hair was disheveled, her mouth caked dry, her face red, but her eyes and ears picked up every movement, every sound around her.

I nudged her arm. She flashed me a quick smile and returned to the mirror. The smile faded as she saw the glint of the forceps. The doctor had them in his hand. The anesthetist moved in.

The midwife leaned over and I could hear her murmuring a few words: "Wait, wait. One more minute. Please, please." The doctor stepped back. He put the forceps on the table behind him. He lowered his eyes. Minutes passed. Yet, they seemed like hours and then his eyes raised and I could see a twinkle ever so slightly starting. "Good, good," I heard him say. "Push easy. Good. I see a quarter's worth. A quarter's worth."

I looked at Nancy. Her face was one of absolute concentration and determination. She watched the doctor's eyes with occasional glances at the instrument behind him. "Easy, good," he continued. "Once more. Push. Hold it." He moved forward and his arms dropped. I didn't look. I closed my eyes and waited. "I've got the cord. I've got it. Good girl. Good girl."

The anesthetist stepped back from the table.

The doctor turned to me. I could see a smile cross his face even behind the mask. "Now, we'll go slow and easy so you can take all the pictures you want."

Did he really say that? To me? Was this being choreographed for me? Was I really that important?

I looked at the clock. 9:30. And then, when I looked back, I heard the doctor's soft, steady words. I heard them

159

but I don't know if I really listened. It seemed like something I could not understand. I had never seen or felt anything like this before, whether in a sleeping dream or in my waking imagination.

"Now, Nancy, here we go. Push only when I tell you. Slow. Count to five. Now, push."

He glanced at me. Quickly, I brought the camera up to my eyes and as soon as I peeked through the viewer, I could see the top of a head, a tiny, slippery wet head followed by a set of eyes—they were opened—a nose, a mouth, a chin. It was all easing into the picture. It was smiling. It was smiling. I remember clicking once, twice, again. Another pair of hands reached into the frame and a tube was inserted into the mouth of that head. The tube was removed and I heard something. I heard someone crying. From where? Who was that?

I looked at Nancy. She was propped up. I was staring at a two-headed being. Her eyes were huge, her mouth was open. She was in a state of disbelief. The doctor's voice came in once more. "All right, slow, now, Nancy. This one has broad shoulders. It's bullying its way out like a billy goat. One shoulder at a time now. Fine. A little more. Fine."

Again my eyes shot up. The baby was halfway into the sunlight. But then the doctor stopped. "Okay, everyone take a breath. Now—" The glint was back in his eyes. "Place your bets, ladies and gentlemen. Place your bets. Is this billy goat a boy or a girl?"

Everyone chuckled. I turned to Nancy. "A boy," we said in unison.

"Here we go."

The bottom half slid out but I didn't see anything. My camera had stopped clicking and I was trying to capture the picture with my eyes. It was a different kind of picture. It was one that I would never forget because it could never yellow or fade or even get lost like a photograph. It was stamped in my mind as part of my memory forever.

The baby was picked up. He—He was crying and smiling and crying and—my God, I can't believe it. I couldn't believe what was happening. My stomach was heaving. My eyes seemed to be coming out of their sockets. My ears were clogging up on me. I was floating somewhere, somehow. Someone was crying and laughing and smiling and crying and . . . who was it? Who was it among us doing all this?

I stood there watching, which was all I could do. I seemed paralyzed, unable to think. I watched as they cleaned him up. I watched as they put him in a warmer. I touched the person next to me. Our eyes were fixed on what was going on across the room. There was another person over there. A new one who wasn't here when we first came into this room. A human being with fingers and toes and ears; everything and we had produced him. We had created him. He was part of us, our tissues, our blood. He was us.

I leaned down and kissed my partner, and I could taste the salt in her tears.

The doctor came to my side and held out his hand. "He's a fine one. Congratulations." I smiled. He took me around the shoulders. "Come on, make a phone call to someone. Give her a chance to get some rest."

We loosened our masks as we pushed the door open. The first whiff of air almost made me giddy. I looked back in the room. The sun was pouring in now. The baby was being cared for by two nurses; Nancy by two more.

Life had begun in that room. Our son's life and perhaps mine too. I walked down the hall. The clock was at ten. Another couple was just being escorted into labor room number two. I nodded at the guy with the white, full-length coat and the goody bag. Is there really any other way?

I sat in the phone booth and dialed the long-distance number.

"Mother, Happy Anniversary. I have some news for you. At 9:34 this morning, there was born a child. Seven pounds, two and a half ounces. The last name is Kahan. The middle name is White and . . ."

I paused. I held my breath and what I had just seen and felt flashed through me again. I thought of my grandfather and I thought of tradition and I thought of what the doctor had said and the sign which Nancy had given me and I thought of love and of people and of giving and of sharing; I could feel it all.

"Happy Anniversary, Mom. And the first name is—Billy."

Summary

Months 7, 8, and 9 are probably the most exciting and the most aggravating. There is no question that they are tension-filled months for it is during this period when you must be at your best: a combination of calmness, understanding, and compassion.

Dr. Wider again: "While the doctor is attuning himself to the couple's needs, the expectant father must attune himself to the expectant mother's needs."

As you have already seen, the physical and emotional demands on you will increase. As birth time approaches, it will be important for you to take the lead in most matters. Remember, the excitement which your mate was feeling during the first six months has now given way to feelings of insecurity and anxiousness, and rightly so.

These will be the times which really test you. Therefore,

you must be able to rise above the pettiness, the silliness, the impractical. You must function on a realistic, practical level, but without giving up the excitement which you may still feel. This is a tough line to walk.

And what of birth? As you can see, my experience is only one. Different men see birth differently: Some want no part of it; some may even want to deliver the child personally. It is all a matter of preference.

But, what does it really come down to? Well, what do you think? Have the past nine months been worth it? Would you do it again?

It's still a question of personal taste, but before you give yourself a quick answer, you should look at one more month. Pregnancy has ended but a new chapter has started. Follow me. You'll see what I mean.

Chapter 4:
The 10th Month

Today you were born, William White Kahan. 9:34 A.M. 7 lbs., 2½ ozs. And you are beautiful. You really are. You're rosy and fair-skinned and dark-haired. And you look so peaceful and calm. All day you've been sleeping and looking around at this strange, new world you've been thrust into. I wonder what you're feeling right now? You have a look about you that reminds me of Daddy. But I think you have my disposition.

Feelings of Becoming a Father

Those are the words Nancy wrote Billy on the first day of his life. They may strike a woman one way and a man another. What do I mean? Well, there are many levels of reactions. A woman may see things in a way you may not. One thing, though, is for sure: A new mother is a possessive individual, even more so than a new father. What is hers is hers, and what is yours is hers, and what is the both of yours, is also hers.

When you consider what she has been through, you can probably understand what the baby means to her. This is not to say that the baby is unimportant to you, but often the extent of the responsibility may differ.

The tenth month is a time of newness, of freshness for both of you. It's a rough month. You'll be tired, scared; your nerves will be frayed. You may be afraid of the baby because you don't know what to do with it or how to take care of it. You may be afraid of these new obligations, pressures, demands. It'll be physically very difficult. You may even be exhausted from being up at night, whether you have been involved in the feeding or not. You will also experience a feeling of being left out. Now, doesn't that seem like enough?

And your relationship with the mother of your child may also be different. When she is not taking care of the baby, she will be tired and not her usual self. She is preoccupied, absorbed to a great extent in the baby, especially during the first couple of weeks. There is a lack of sleep, there are the growing anxieties: When do I know the baby is sick? When do I call the doctor. What do I do?

As a couple, you may also be knocked out moneywise, particularly if she had been working at the time, but may not want to go back too soon, if at all. You may now be the sole moneymaker, as in our case where both of us had top jobs and each had contributed substantially to the running of the household.

The situation can be frightening. You will feel left out, jealous, perhaps annoyed that you can no longer do the things you did two weeks ago, like going to a movie, a restaurant, even a walk around the block late at night.

It is a feeling of being cut off, weighed down. In many ways, it's harder for you because the woman, while she has hormonal changes, also has the intense deep feelings of the closeness of the baby just by the fact of giving birth; you may have none of these things, even if you had been involved in the labor and delivery process. It is still not the same thing as the mother/child relationship.

There is nothing abnormal about any of the above feelings. But the key, as we said in the opening pages of this book, is *involvement*, in projecting yourself into the picture as much as possible. Try to arrange to take off from work the first week the baby is home. Pick up a feeding at least once a day. It won't hurt and I daresay when your son or daughter is resting in your arms, the body against your chest, perhaps grasping one of your fingers with his or her entire hand and looking up into your eyes, you might just get a feeling come over you that you have never experienced before. Try it, you'll like it!

Also, it is important for the couple to get out as soon as possible. Try to arrange for a baby-sitter sometime within the first month so you and your wife can go out to dinner or a movie or a show.

There are certain practical and emotional aspects of having a new person in your house. However, it is not the intention of this section to delve into every facet of the daily activities of your new baby. If you need to know specifics, you should be asking your pediatrician. In fact, remember to call him right after the birth so that he can come to the hospital and examine the baby. Additionally, there are a number of books on baby care available which you can refer to if need be and, as previously mentioned, the Spock and Gersh books are two of the best.

Instead of repeating what has already been written in much greater detail elsewhere, let's generally look at some of the things which the new father (and that's what you are now) will see and feel at this time.

The Baby and You
Baby's Looks

You will undoubtedly notice that your new son or daughter looks nothing like the Gerber ads. This is not unusual. A newborn is not usually exactly a thing of beauty. Expect to see a large head which may resemble a cucumber, perhaps a flattened nose, blotchy and scaly skin, swollen genitals, and chicken legs. All quite normal. Don't be scared. The head will eventually become rounder, the nose will straighten, the skin will become soft and smooth, the genitals will reduce to their proportionate size, and those legs will begin to look like legs.

If you see blue eyes on your baby and both you and your wife have brown eyes (remember the genetics chart?), don't get excited too quickly. Most newborns have blue eyes but the color will usually change in time . . . or they could remain the same. This also applies to hair coloring. A blonde-haired baby at birth could very easily become a dark-haired child within six months.

Baby's Food

For the first month, you needn't defrost that small sirloin for your new son. He won't be eating it for quite some time. His diet will be mainly milk and perhaps a liquid vitamin supplement. The milk can either be from the breast or via the bottle in the way of formula. There are advantages and disadvantages to each, but you should be checking with the pediatrician as to what is best for you, depending on what you and the mother want.

Baby's Physical Condition

There are certain things about a baby which will be new to you and, therefore, worrying is a natural part of your daily diet. Why? Because you may not have the knowledge to stop from worrying.

Let's take a few examples:

Sneezing.   You will find that a baby sneezes a lot. How much is not really important unless it is constant. But the purpose of a baby sneezing is to clean his nose from dust and other particles. Remember, a baby doesn't know about asking for Kleenex yet.

Grunting.   A baby will make various animal sounds such as cooing, mumbling, grunting, growling, even hic-cupping. All quite normal. Some of these sounds could be the result of a gas bubble; some could be a primitive form of communication. Research is still being done on this latter aspect, but evidence thus far has shown that infants (even those fresh from the womb) do show signs of communicat-ing and one of these ways is by vocal noises.

Weight Loss.   A newborn usually will lose on the average of a half-pound to a pound from the time of birth to the time he comes home. Why? The weight loss is due to evaporation of body water and it is common in all babies. Don't be too concerned. He'll gain it back and then some. In fact, figure that in four months, he will double his weight.

Immunity.   An infant is pretty much immune from colds and other diseases for at least the first three months of life. This immunity is passed on by the mother. Actually, in breast-fed babies, it is reported that the immunity lasts for as long as six months. Of course, this does not give you a license to go hog-wild and expose your new infant to people with colds or to place him in a position where the likelihood of his picking up a disease is good.

Temperature and Comfort.   Generally, a newborn likes an atmosphere which is somewhat similar to the womb; that is, on the warmer side. This is one of the reasons the infant is placed in a warmer immediately after birth. Accordingly, keep the baby's room at around seventy-two degrees for the first few weeks.

You can also be guided somewhat by yourself. Babies will pretty much respond to their environment. If the temperature is comfortable to you (provided you don't find sitting in your underwear in twenty-degree weather your idea of heaven), it will by and large satisfy the baby.

Breathing Patterns. It is recommended that the baby does not sleep in the same room as you. Why? A baby's breathing pattern is quite different from yours. His is basically an irregular one with twitches, snorts, reflexes of all sorts, and occasional cries. (Oh, that's yours too?) This can be quite unsettling at night.

Incidentally, for the first few weeks a baby breathes through his nose. He hasn't learned to breathe through his mouth yet. Therefore, as one other tip, try to keep the smokers out of his room. How would you feel if you could only breathe through your nose and that was clogged with cigar smoke? Usually, if it's not right for you, it won't be right for the baby.

Fresh Air. Nothing like it. Our doctor recommended that we take our newborn out for a stroll as soon as the weather permitted. But, use your head. If *you* wouldn't go out, then don't take the baby out. And when you do, do it prudently. A little bit at a time, like when you have the whole summer to get a tan: ten minutes the first day, fifteen minutes the second, slowly increasing the time. By the same token, although fresh air is good for a baby, try to restrict your visiting other people during the first couple of weeks. Let the people come to you instead. In short, don't shlep the baby around too much.

Crying. Forget all the words and old wives' tales, especially the word "colic." Don't listen to everybody or figure that your kid has what the neighbor's kid had.

When a baby cries, it is pretty much for a specific reason. Either he's wet or uncomfortable in some way, or he's hungry or he's got a little gas. That's principally it. Pick him up. You won't spoil him. All he may need is a little warmth, a little loving, a little comfort. Remember where he's been for the past nine months? Use some common sense. A baby can't fend for itself. How would you feel if you were thirsty in the middle of the night and you couldn't get yourself a glass of water?

This leads us logically into two more aspects: sleeping and feeding.

Sleeping. For the first month, a baby usually will be asleep more than he will be awake. Figure that the sleep cycle will be on a three to four hour basis; that is, you can expect your offspring to pop awake within those hours. Some babies require less sleep, some more, but four is the average. Why does the baby get up so often? Because he's hungry.

Feeding. There are two concepts of feeding: Demand-feeding, which means when the baby demands, you feed; and fixed- or forced-feeding, which means you feed the baby on a fixed schedule, even if you have to wake him to do it. The kind of feeding you will do depends on your philosophy in raising your child. In any event, discuss this with your doctor.

Picking the Baby Up. One thing to keep in mind: A baby is not that fragile. They are hardier than most people like to believe. So don't be afraid to pick that baby up, to cuddle it, to play with it. However, do watch the head. I mean, don't worry about it falling off and rolling across the floor. That won't happen, but the head, if you don't give it

171

some support, could wind up lolling about on your shoulder and think how you would feel if your head was hanging one way with your body another.

There are a few ways you can carry a baby and they are relatively easy ones. For example, one useful way is in one arm, called the "football carry." Know how you grip a football lengthwise in one arm? That's the same way you could carry the baby. No, I am not joking. This technique is an authorized, recommended one by the Red Cross. The important thing is to give the infant support. That shouldn't present any problem. He's only around seven pounds. You can't hold that?

Remember again, babies are quite resilient. Don't be frightened of them. They won't break. Besides, if you show tension, the baby will feel it.

Sight. As I said before, a baby does see at birth. Although the sharpness of his sight may be suspect, he does have vision and can distinguish quite easily between what is moving and what is not.

During this tenth month, you will obviously be on the receiving end of countless suggestions, recommendations, and advice on how to raise your child. In fact, the amount will double that of what was offered you during the pregnancy months. Here is where you must be guided by your own common sense and instincts. For example, how can you swallow the advice given by the child psychiatrist down the hall when his kid is a holy terror? Or, how can you listen to Aunt Violet when her kid was born for sitting in a corner, urinating, and finger-painting the walls? Listen to yourself. You probably have a better and clearer understanding of what is best for your child.

If you're looking for some practical tips and answers to some specific questions, try these:

1. *Is the newborn really a blob*? On the contrary. You would be surprised at what a newborn can do. An infant shows excitement, distress, smiles, responds, adjusts itself position-wise, and recognizes voices. In short, don't sell your kid short. *Tip*: Smiling starts early. It's not all gas. Speak softly. Coo. A father's voice is especially soothing to a baby and the combination of that voice and the father's natural playfulness may become a favorite of the baby.

2. *During fussy periods, why does a baby respond to motion*? It may remind him of being back in his mother. *Tip*: Try walking him or using a rocker. Carriage rides will also pacify him.

Note: A baby will sometimes become fretful if you are. In other words, if you are tense, a baby will feel it. Relax, even if you have to take a drink after a hard day's work, but do it *before* you pick the baby up.

3. *What happens to my sex life*? What happens to what? I think you can pretty much answer that by now. Usually the woman will have an examination four to six weeks after the delivery. By then, everything should be healed and the green flag should be waved. *Tip*: While we're on the subject, as a prelude to sex, make some arrangement to get away (the two of you) by the end of the first month. I mentioned it earlier; I'm now repeating it for emphasis. Hire a baby-sitter and get out for a dinner and/or some form of entertainment. Although your family is now three instead of two, remember, the baby should not replace your relationship with your mate.

4. *Aren't there plenty of don'ts relating to the baby*? Sure. For example:

a. *Don't* leave the infant alone in an unprotected place, such as on a dressing table.

b. *Don't* give the baby a bottle by propping it up on a

pillow or something similar. Always hold the baby when feeding him.

c. *Don't* just plunk a bottle in the baby's mouth without making sure it's the right temperature. A baby won't care for milk right out of the freezer, or which has just been boiled.

d. *Don't* leave small, swallowable objects such as safety pins and rings near the baby. They will wind up in his mouth faster than you think.

e. *Don't* use pillows in the crib. Not only is it unnecessary, but it is dangerous.

f. *Don't* be overly concerned about spitting up and bowel movements. Spitting up is perfectly normal as long as the baby is otherwise happy. The same holds true for the frequency or infrequency of a bowel movement. Americans, in particular, are noted for their obsession with toilet habits. If something is bothering you, however, check with the doctor.

g. *Don't* stick things in the baby's ears or nose. The internal organs here are quite sensitive and you could easily puncture an eardrum without realizing it.

h. *Don't* leave appliances nearby when you are doing something with the baby, especially when it has to do with water. For example, having a radio sitting on the edge of the tub while you're bathing the baby. Don't laugh. This is not an unusual occurrence.

5. *Aren't there plenty of do's? Sure.*

    a. *Do* give that baby love.

    b. *Do* snuggle him.

    c. *Do* coo with him.

    d. *Do* kiss him.

    e. *Do* play with him.

    f. *Do* enjoy him.

So, was it all worth it? Would you do it again? That's for you to answer. As for me, I have my own opinion. I formed it after the first month, after the newness and tension had worn off, after I realized what was still to come: the crazy things and the good things, the fun things and the agonizing things, the fears and the challenges. It came to me one night during the latter part of November.

Billy was now a month old. It was 2:30 in the morning, a Monday morning no less. The two o'clock feeding was over; I had taken it. My wife was sleeping and Billy had also just drifted off. He was good that way: no fussing, no carrying on. Drank his milk, burped, and was gone. Maybe it was the calm, quiet pregnancy he was a part of. Maybe it was the natural childbirth. Maybe it was us. Maybe it was a combination of all those things.

I put him down and watched as the eyes fluttered shut, the clenched fists relaxed and opened, the body coming at ease.

There he was, all serene in a blue stretch suit with his stuffed animals within eye range: Mr. Lion and Mr. Turtle and Lambie and Raggedy Andy and good old Mickey Mouse.

I looked down at him. It was just beginning. We were at the starting gate again: the crawling, the walking, the running, the talking, the laughing. It would not be long before he and I would be in the park throwing a football around or bicycling to the nearest hot dog stand or just sitting on the couch next to each other eating chocolate chip cookies and watching a cartoon.

He was part of me and it was as if I had been reborn again. At age forty, I now had my life extended by the presence of this little fellow who bore my name and some of my features. It's strange to talk about, because it's such a personal thing. But, yet, we do, because sharing is also part of our being.

So, does that answer the question? For me it did, especially when I felt it come down the side of my face and then drop onto the cheek below.

The eyes opened ever so slightly at what had awakened them, and then they closed and I swear . . . I swear I could see a flicker of a smile skip across that face.

Index

Afterbirth, 121, 150
 see also Placenta
Akmakjian, Dr. Haig, *The
 Natural Way to Raise a
 Healthy Child*, 31
American Society for Psycho-
 Prophylaxis in Obstetrics,
 110
Amniocentesis, 121, 128–129
Amniotic fluid, *see* Waters,
 bag of
Analgesics in childbirth, 88,
 121
Anesthetics in childbirth, 88,
 121
Anxieties of parents-to-be, 98–
 102
Apgar Test, 121–122

Birth
 methods listed, 86–93
 participation of husband in,
  91–92, 117–121, 157–
  161
 use of drugs in, 87–88, 90
 see also Lamaze Method;
  Leboyer; Natural birth
Body build, genetics of, 132,
 135–136
Breast
 development, 43
 feeding, 48–49, 169
Breathing
 patterns of newborn, 170
 techniques for birth, 110–
  111, 114–119, 147, 156
Breech birth, 122

Caesarean, 86, 89–90
Caput, 122
Cervix, 122
 dilation of, 122, 146–148
 effacement, 123
 mucous plug, 124

177

Chin shape, genetics of, 135
Circumcision, 66
Classes for expectant parents,
    64, 92, 110, 145
Clinics, obstetrical, 25
Clothes
    baby, 66, 138, 142–143
    maternity, 58–63
Color as stimulus for baby,
    141
Communication, husband-
    wife, 39, 102
Contractions, 145, 146–148,
    151
    Braxton-Hicks, 122, 146
    see also Labor
Costs, see Financial aspects
Couvade, 5
Crowning, 122
Crying of newborn, 170–171

Delivery, 157–161
    emergency instructions for,
        148–150
    see also, Birth
Demerol, 122
Dental problems, 47
Diet, see Nutrition
Dimples, genetics of, 135
Dipping, 122
Drinking during pregnancy, 34
Drugs, use in labor, 87–88,
    121, 122, 123

Effacement, 123
Emotional changes during
    pregnancy, 31–40
Employment during preg-
    nancy, 47, 65
Engagement, 123, 146
Episiotomy, 123
Exercise, 74–79
    in Lamaze Method, 109,
        112–118
Eye color, genetics of, 129–
    130, 133, 168

Fetus
    development, 27, 42, 69,
        94, 104, 145
    heart rate (F.H.R.), 123
    monitor, 123, 156
    movements, 105–107
Financial aspects, 23–26, 47,
    64–67, 141
Floating, 123
Food crazes, 50–51
Forceps, 86, 88–89, 123
Freckles, genetics of, 134
Friends, reactions of, 15–17
Fundus, 123
Furniture, baby, 66, 140, 143

Genetics, 125–136
Gennaro, Peter, on exercise,
    74
Gersh, Marvin J., *How to
    Raise Children at Home
    in Your Spare Time*, 144
Gifts for baby, 143
Glossary of obstetrical terms,
    121–125

Goody bag, 118–119
Grandparents-to-be, 13–15, 20
Green, Maureen, *Fathering*, 12
Guttmacher, Dr. Alan G., *Pregnancy, Birth and Family Planning*, 30, 108
Gynecologist, 18

Hair, genetics of, 132, 133–134
Head shape, genetics of, 131
Height, genetics of, 132, 135–136
Hospital
  charges, 24, 25, 66
  confinement policies of, 21–22
  route to, 141
Housework, helping with, 68

Immunity of newborn, 169
Insurance coverage for obstetrics, 24–25, 65
Irritability during pregnancy, 99

Jealousy of expectant father, 99–101

Kallop, Fritzi, 64, 110

Labor, 88, 146–158
  induction of, 87, 123, 124
  onset of, 145–146
  phases of, 123

premature, 124
stages of, 124
transition, 125
see also Delivery
Lactation, 48
Lamaze Method, 91, 109–117, 147, 156
Lanugo, 95
Leboyer, Dr. Frederick
  Birth Without Violence, 93–94
  Leboyer Method, 93–94

Midwife, 25, 87, 90–91
Milinaire, Caterine, *Birth*, 31
Miscarriage, 70
Moodiness during pregnancy, 36–40
Morning sickness, 42
Mouth shape, genetics of, 135
Movement of fetus, 105–107
Musiker, Dr. Seymour, 139–140

Naming the baby, 79–86
Natalins, 48
Natural birth, 22, 86–87, 92–93, 108–109, 118–121
  see also Lamaze Method
Nausea, 42
Newborn, characteristics and handling of, 168–173
Nose shape, genetics of, 130–131, 135
Nurse, 66, 140

The Expectant Father's Survival Kit

Nutrition
  for baby, 168, 171
  for expectant mother, 48–54

Obstetrical terms, definitions
    of, 121–125
Obstetrician, 18
  fees, 23, 66
  relation to father, 22–26
  selection of, 18–23
Occiput posterior, 124
Old wives' tales, 31–35, 125
O'Mansky, Dr. Boris L., 118,
    139

Pediatrician
  fees, 66
  selection of, 138–139
Pelvimetry, 124
Perineum, 124
Photography of birth, 119
Physical characteristics of
    child, 129–136
Physical and psychological
    changes, 42–47, 67, 69,
    95, 97, 145–146
  in father-to-be, 45–46
Pitocin, 123
Placenta, 124
  see also Afterbirth
Premature labor, 124
Prenatal checkups, frequency
    of, 23
Preparation for Parenthood
    Program, 64, 92, 110
Princeton Center for Infancy

and Early Childhood,
    The First Twelve Months
    of Life, 144

Quickening, 124

Reading materials
  on baby care, 126–127, 144
  on pregnancy, 28–31
Room for baby, 140–141, 169
Rooming-in, 22

Safety precautions, 141–142
Salk, Dr. Lee, Preparing for
    Parenthood, 2
Scheinfeld, Amram, Your
    Heredity and Environ-
    ment, 129
Sex of baby, 79, 125–129,
    136–137
Sexual relations, 40–43, 69–
    73, 102–104
  postnatal, 173
Skin color, genetics of, 134
Sleeping habits
  of baby, 171
  of expectant mother, 46–47,
    67
Sneezing of newborn, 169
Sonogram, 124
Sphincter, 124
Spock, Dr. Benjamin, Baby
    and Child Care, 144

Tax deductions, 67

Index

Temperature, body, during
    pregnancy, 45–46
Temperature, room, for new-
    born, 169
Toiletries for baby, 138, 143
Twilight sleep, 87
Twins or more, 69, 128, 136

Umbilical cord, 149, 150

Vernix, 95, 125
Vertex, 125
Vitamins, 48–49

Vocal noises by baby, 169

Wagner, Frank, *Body Works*,
    79
Waters, bag of, 122, 145, 153–
    154
Weight of baby, 132, 136, 169
Weight changes
    of expectant father, 48, 54
    of expectant mother, 54, 67
Wider, Jerry A., 120–121
Wright, Erna, *The New Child-
    birth*, 115